Advance Pr

"Sometimes a way to gauge ... quality of a creation is to think about what it took, what was overcome, what price it extracted. In this case, the proof is in your hands. It is raw and palpable and beats like a heart. He gave everything he had: infinite strength, exacting discipline, fearsome courage. When you put this book down, trust me, you will think about it for a long time."

—Robert Olmstead, author of the national bestseller *Coal Black Horse*

"James Brown has shaped from the English language something rather different: an exacting, muscular prose both tender and unforgiving, rigorously concise in its refusal to dilute the darkest realities and yet capacious and nuanced in its pursuit of redemption and familial love. He is one of our most accomplished writers, and this brilliant memoir is among the finest of its kind."

—B.H. Fairchild, author of the National Book Critics Circle Award winning *Early Occult Memory Systems of the Lower Midwest*, and National Book Award nominated *The Art of the Lathe*

"This is a harrowing and beautiful memoir, shot through with excess and violence and shocking, heart-stopping compassion. James Brown renders his extraordinary life in tight, muscular prose, sparing neither himself nor the reader the hard lessons of addiction and recovery. The result is an unforgettable book, stripped of irony and pretense that lays bare the darkness—and the light—in all of us."

—Bret Anthony Johnston, author of *Corpus Christi: Stories*

"James Brown's provocative, beautifully written and gut wrenching memoir illuminates a life rich in those elemental passions that govern our lives—anger, fear, depression, death, and love. Sometimes tender, sometimes manic, but always wise and insightful, *This River* never falters in the muscularity of the writing, all of it filled with riveting details that kept this reader turning the pages as fast as he could read them. Here is a remarkable life, one that is both devastating and inspiring. Any ordinary man experiencing what Brown went through would doubtless have died long ago, but Brown not only survived, he triumphed and in ways no one would have predicted, least of all, perhaps, Brown himself. Mesmerizing from beginning to end. Unforgettable."

—Duff Brenna, author of *The Book of Mamie*, winner of the AWP Award for Best Novel, and *Too Cool*, a New York Times Notable Book of the Year

"Sequel to Brown's indelible *The Los Angeles Diaries*, this cycle of linked narratives is equally powerful and complete in itself. Brown's profoundly authentic story of Brown, survivor of sibling suicides, drinker, user, writer, teacher, father, husband, is as fully imagined as it is unsparing. In speaking from the edge of loss, Brown's eloquence recalls Robert Lowell's 'this eye has seen what this hand has done.'"

—DeWitt Henry, author of *Safe Suicide*

Praise for *The Los Angeles Diaries*

"*The Los Angeles Diaries* is one of those rare memoirs that cuts deeply, chillingly into the reader's own dreams. It is a dramatic, vivid, heartbreaking, very personal story of human responsibility and guilt, of alcoholism, of suicide, of marital struggle, of the uncertainties and ambiguities of a writer's life in modern America. The book is cleanly and beautifully written, and it's also incredibly moving."

—Tim O'Brien, author of *The Things They Carried*

"*The Los Angeles Diaries* is terrific. It's one of the toughest memoirs I've ever read, at once spare and startlingly, admirably unsparing. It glows with a dark luminescence. James Brown is a fine, fine writer."

—**Michael Chabon, Pulitzer Prize winning author of** *The Amazing Adventures of Kavalier & Clay* **and** *The Yiddish Policemen's Union*

"This gemlike collection…materializes in such delicate strokes that the emerging theme becomes one of almost miraculous forgiveness, any pain and rage all but hidden between the lines."

—*San Francisco Chronicle* **(Best Books of the Year)**

"Profound…unsparing and clear-eyed, a heartbreaking story, and yet oddly inspirational, the tale of the last man standing."

—**Janet Fitch**

"Life-affirming…. An extraordinarily gripping, honest, and somehow uplifting tale. It seamlessly moves from bleak to beautiful…. A darkly bright, hugely compassionate, and oddly redemptive story of loss and failure, guilt and addiction."

—*The Independent*

"As tragic as Brown's life has been, the memoir displays neither pathos nor self-pity but elegiac wisdom...How moving is Brown's *The Los Angeles Diaries*? While double-checking the quotes and facts, I simply gave in and reread it again, struck even more by its pain, its beauty and its craft."

—**Deirdre Donahue,** *USA Today*

"It's the balance of agony and grace, of course, that makes life so ferociously interesting. Brown has perfectly captured that balance in this unpretentious, very profound book."

—**Carolyn See,** *Washington Post*

"Novelist Brown (Lucky Town; Hot Wire; etc.) mines the explosive territory of his own harsh and complicated life in this gut-wrenching memoir.... Brown flays open his own tortured skin looking for what blood beats beneath and why. The result is a grimly exquisite memoir that reads like a noir novel but grips unrelentingly like the hand of a homeless drunk begging for help."

—Publishers Weekly

"Brown's blackout days make for a darkly alluring read. This is the kind of book that becomes an underground classic for all the wrong reasons."

—Booklist

"...a riveting read. A supremely powerful and depressing memoir, then, one that seeks to evoke and express—rather than in any way explain—the misery that engulfed one ambitious American family."

—Kirkus

"This is a ghost story, and James Brown should be dead. That he is not is a remarkable tale of perseverance in the face of staggering loss and tragedy."

—Charles Feldman, CNN

"Remarkable...Rises above the commonplace to the true art of comprehended pain...the hallmark of Brown's prose is gravitas. His truths are definitive"

—DeWitt Henry, Boston Globe

"*Searing, gut-churning but ultimately luminous...The Los Angeles Diaries* reads like the best – and darkest – fiction...Uncompromisingly bleak yet surprisingly beautiful, a passionate testament not only to how one can survive what should shatter and sunder irreparably, but that one can survive and in surviving, begin anew."

—Baltimore Sun

This River

By James Brown

Library of Congress Catalog Information Available

Book Design by Marti Lou Critchfield

Printed in the Canada

Phoenix Books, Inc.
9465 Wilshire Boulevard, Suite 840
Beverly Hills, CA 90212

10 9 8 7 6 5 4 3 2 1

For Paula

Of this book, earlier versions of chapters appeared in: "This River" and "Dirty Moves" in the *Los Angeles Times Magazine.* The latter piece was also reprinted in *Best American Sports Writing* (Houghton Mifflin) and *Fathers and Sons and Sports: An Anthology of Great American Sports Writing* (ESPN Books). "Some Kind of Animal" was published in *GQ* under the title "The Beast in Me," "Talking to the Dead," appeared in the *Santa Monica Review,* "Instructions on the Use of Alcohol" was published in *Redivider: A Journal of New Literature* under the title "How Some of Us Become Drunks and Junkies", and "Blood and Duplicity" appeared in *Ploughshares* under the title "Missing the Dead."

CONTENTS

Talking to the Dead

There's another side to this story, when my brother and sister visit late at night, or in the early morning hours, and we simply talk. They are glad to see me again, as I am glad to see them, and we like to catch up on things. If only for a brief while, I am dreaming my brother and sister alive, and I'm grateful for their company.

Other times I'll wake up shouting, the tips of my hair damp with sweat. Paula says that when I sleep my legs are like live wires. She even writes a poem about it. A dark poem about nightmares and personal demons. Afterwards, I'll lay in bed for hours, afraid to close my eyes. Add to the mix my long-standing battle with depression and I'm blessed with what in the field of psychopathology is regarded as a deeply disturbed mind. These are the things that inspire Paula to put such personal matters to paper. We're married by this time, and I suppose, in some ways, that gives her the right.

Not a day goes by where I don't think of my dead brother and sister, my dead father, too, and now, most recently, my dead ex-wife. I could be in the middle of a conference with a student at the college where I teach and it'll flash on me, my brother, recoiling from the gun shot that took his life. I could be driving home and I'll see my sister sprawled out on the concrete bank of the Los Angeles River, her limbs twisted in all the wrong directions. I try not to imagine her bleeding. I try to blank out how the blood drains, the pool widening around her. The fall from the overpass wasn't more than twenty-five, thirty feet, and I doubt she died on impact. The skull, I'm sure it cracked, but the heart may have continued to pulse. I pray she went into shock quickly, and alive or not, for however long she possibly lingered, that mercifully she soon felt nothing. And I cannot pass a hospital, any hospital, without hearing the sickening thump-and-hiss of the ventilator on which both my father and ex-wife spent their final days, unable to speak.

I try to forget these things.

I try to push them out of my thoughts.

If it's during the day, and I drink enough, I'll sometimes succeed. But at night when I fall asleep, as the alcohol wears off and the subconscious comes into play, all bets are off. My brother shot himself in bed, and often my dreams fuse with memory, so that I find myself reliving a heightened version of the actual experience, cleaning up his room after the suicide, etching into my mind images of crystallized blood and fragments of bone. These dreams, or visions, whatever you'd like to call them, unroll frame-by-frame, in glimpses and flashes, and for years they've kept me from countless hours of sleep.

Time after time the dream that begins with promise quickly grows dark, and I'm returned to consciousness by Paula shaking me, shouting, "wake up, wake up." Eventually her patience wears thin, and one morning over coffee, she confronts me.

"You need to get help."

"What do you mean?"

"You know exactly what I mean." She reaches across the kitchen table and touches my temple with her fingers. "It's a circus in there, and you don't even see it. I'm worried. I've been worried a long time, Jim, and I really don't know how much more you can take of this?" She only uses my name when she wants to instruct, and her tone is sincere. "Every night you drink until you pass out because you can't sleep, but the drinking only makes the nightmares worse. Something has to give," she says. "There must be some kind of medication you can take."

Medication, I think, is for the truly troubled psyche, and I don't see myself quite that far down the line. And strangely enough for an alcoholic-slash-addict, I don't want to get strung out on whatever some doctor might prescribe. Depression and nightmares, however, frequently go hand-in-hand, and I figure that if I can remedy one, I'm bound to see improvement in the other. I'm also not altogether enamored by the idea of bearing my soul to a psychiatrist, so in my initial plan of attack I make an appointment with a general practitioner. On my first visit I tell him that I'm depressed.

"Have you had a recent crisis?" he asks.

"The loss of a loved one, your job, a divorce?"

"Not recently," I say.

"But you've been depressed?"

"Yes."

"For how long?"

"A couple years."

It's been much longer, but I don't want to make a bigger deal out of this than it already is, so I lie. And it's that easy. Ten minutes later I'm out the door with a prescription in my pocket, cautiously hopeful that maybe, just maybe, these pills might work.

This day marks the beginning of my journey through the world of psychotropic antidepressants. In the months to follow, through the tedious process of trial and error, I learn that what lifts the dark clouds from around the psyche of one troubled soul may in fact cause a hail storm in another. As millions of others before me, I start with Prozac, and inside of a week I find that it does take the edge off my depression. But it also takes the edge off every other feeling, from joy to anger, and I find myself living in a haze of emotional mediocrity. Even worse, I can't get it up in the bedroom, and as a result I sink into a depression uglier than the one I'm trying to shake.

I return to the doctor.

This time he prescribes Zoloft, a close cousin to Prozac in the family of antidepressants known as serotonin reuptake inhibitors, or simply SSRI's. It helps with my depression, but again I'm an utter failure in the bedroom. Next on the list is Effexor, chemically different than its predecessors but equally effective in the treatment of chronic despair, and though I don't suffer for it sexually, it raises my already elevated blood pressure to even more dangerous levels. Then comes Serzone, an antidepressant in a class all its own, but it renders me almost completely incapacitated with a constant, shrill-pitched ringing in my ears.

By now nearly a year has passed, and I've just about given up hope of ever finding any relief in the form of a pill, when as a last resort my doctor suggests Wellbutrin, yet another antidepressant but one typically prescribed only after all the others have been tried and failed. The primary reason for caution is the high rate of seizure in its users, but for me, as it turns out, it's a drug well worth the risk. It relieves the gloominess. It gives me energy and improves my mood. Had I been honest with the doctor on the first visit when I filled out the questionnaire in the waiting room, the one asking whether or not I use or have ever used narcotics, I could've saved myself a lot of needless misery. As it turns out, Wellbutrin is often prescribed for those of us who've used too much cocaine, for too long, or any of the various amphetamines. In doing so we've damaged our brain's ability to produce dopamine, one of three neurotransmitters responsible for a feeling of well-being, frequently condemning the worst of us, the hardcore abusers, to a lifelong mental slump.

My search for the right antidepressant ends well, but as far as the nightmares go, they remain unfazed through the entire ordeal. In some ways they've actually grown worse, and several months after the unnecessary death of my former wife, I finally snap. Soon, I wind up in a hospital for people of my condition, those who are suddenly unable to cope, who drink and use too much, what California police refer to as a "fifty-one-fifty" call.

I'm immediately sedated with heavy doses of Valium, and Clonodine for high blood pressure, for it has skyrocketed in the early stages of withdrawal, and my memory of my first days here are a blur. But as the doctors slowly reduce the dosages of my sedatives, my brother and sister pay me a visit. He's the same as I last remember him, as he always is, frozen in time at the age of twenty-seven, forever young and handsome. For my sister, who took her life at forty-four, and who hasn't been gone nearly as long, I see her much as she'd probably look today had she chosen to carry on. You'd think it would come up in conversation, how it is that Marilyn and I have aged while our brother remains young, but it never does. Somehow we all assume it's the natural order of things in the netherworld of life-after-death, and yet I still see myself as the youngest, not physically but in terms of my rank and title as little brother. That role is one of respect and deference, and so I typically listen more than I talk.

In this dream, I'm sitting on the couch in the living room of my brother's last residence, an old run-down house in a poor Los Angeles neighborhood known as Echo Park. My sister is seated beside me. Barry reclines in a beat-up La-Z-Boy, flipping through the pages of a screenplay. I'm not certain, but I believe it's the script for *Piranha*, a low-budget B-movie, the last he ever worked in. He hands me the script.

"Read this," he says.

In yellow highlighter, he's marked off the dialogue of a security guard, and the language strikes me as stiff and artificial. I shake my head.

"Bad, huh?"

"Terrible," I say.

I pass the script to Marilyn, and you can tell by the look on her face that she doesn't think much of it, either.

"Now watch this," he says.

Marilyn grins, because she used to act, too, and knows what's coming. I'm in the dark. Barry stands up from the La-

Z-Boy, and inside of a minute he's taken those stiff, forced lines and made them credible without altering a single word. It's a small but impressive performance interspersed with gestures, movements, and just the right inflections of voice.

Marilyn applauds. I do the same.

"You can't change the lines. You can't rewrite someone else's story. But there's ways of making it better. It's about improvising, Jimmy. It's about *reinventing*," he says, "and letting go."

I wake up then.

My breathing is even and calm, and later that afternoon I meet with one of the staff psychiatrists. Paula has been called in to accompany me. In this uncertain period of my middle years, and more or less a mental wreck, my resolve to keep my private life private has weakened in light of the risk I've become to myself. I worry that if I'm not careful, if I don't watch out, I could easily become a permanent member in my own dream world of the dead. And I can't do that. I have my sons. I have a wife who sees in me what I've lost the ability to see in myself: that I'm something more than a drunk, someone worth saving.

He asks for my story, and for the most part I tell him straight up. Paula, however, isn't about to let me slide and frequently interjects, elaborating on what I persist in minimizing, embellishing on what I diminish. The doctor's diagnoses, when all is said and done, is bipolar disorder and post-traumatic stress disorder. He further speculates that I may be mildly schizophrenic, given my family history of depression and suicide, my tendency toward rage, and the fact that my mother was also once diagnosed as being mentally ill.

"Like alcoholism," he says, "it's a genetic illness, passed down from one generation to the next. We know this now. The studies are irrefutable. But what we didn't have before, and what we have today, are the better medications to treat it."

True or not, I resist the idea that mental illness and alcoholism are somehow inborn. Accepting that premise means embracing the notion of fate, and I don't. I prefer to believe that I'm in full control. That life is in no way predetermined by some flawed pairing of genes and chromosomes. And again, when medication is recommended, I balk at the idea, not wanting, oddly enough, to get hooked on whatever it is he thinks I should take. In this case, it's a powerful antipsychotic drug called Seroquel, and the mere suggestion of it possibly helping prompts a deep sigh of relief from my wife.

"I don't know about this," I say.

"He said it'll help you sleep," my wife tells me. "Why can't you at least try it?"

Understandably so, she is tired of being jolted awake by my dreams. Understandably so, she is tired of always having to follow me up to bed, because I'm afraid to be alone, afraid of where my mind may take me. She, too, is worn down from my dreams, from rarely getting a full night's rest, and on several occasions I've apparently even struck her in my sleep, though I recall nothing about it. So for my wife, as well as myself, I agree to try the medication.

It's strong, this Seroquel, and I'm still in the process of adjusting to it when they release me from the hospital. In that first week home, about thirty minutes after I take the stuff, and I only take it at night, I have difficulty coordinating my arms and legs. Navigating the stairs up to bed is a real test. My wife trails close behind, and once I'm safely in bed, when I attempt to speak, the words come out garbled. My tongue feels thick and fat. Somehow, through grimaces and gibberish, I'm able to communicate my frustration with Seroquel. She gently places her hand on my shoulder and rubs it.

"Relax," she says. "The psychiatrist told us it would take a while for your nervous system to adapt. We just have to give it a chance."

We, I think. Right. She's not the one transformed into a babbling idiot every night. By the end of the week, however, my brain quits misfiring, and I haven't had a single nightmare. The mechanism by which this drug works is unknown, but it's believed to act as an antagonist on a number of different brain receptors. It's prescribed for psychotic disorders, in particular schizophrenia, and by and large it proves a mixed blessing. Though it provides me with a well overdue respite from my own troubled mind, it doesn't distinguish between the good dreams, or visits, and the unwelcome ones, and in the end I'm left with a certain emptiness. A certain longing for the company of the dead.

On the morning of my seventh day home, I awake to bright sunlight. If I've had any dreams, I don't remember them, and I guess that's the whole point. Still I miss them, the dead, knowing I may never be able to dream them alive again. I sit up in bed. My wife stands beside the bedroom window, pulling back the drapes. She's considerably younger than me, and she looks unburdened, even hopeful. The sunlight is on her face. The sunlight is in her brown hair and she is staring out the window into the woods. I get up. I walk over to her and slip my arms around her.

She leans back into me, and for once in a very long while I'm there, really there, seeing what she sees. The tall pines and cedars, and beyond them a denser forest.

Blood and Duplicity

She's already fallen twice, first breaking the left hip when she misses a step at the beauty parlor, then her right in a tumble at her old house in Arizona. It's in this precarious condition that my mother comes back into my life. When her second husband dies, it falls on me, as her only surviving child, to move her from Arizona to the Shandin Hills Retirement Community in San Bernardino where I can better attend to her needs. She is eighty-two. I am forty-seven. My mother and I have never been close. There are many reasons for this, but chief among them is my brother's suicide, the accompanying guilt, and my need to blame, and in large part I blamed her. For nearly twenty years, we rarely spoke. Now, for the first time in my adult life, I am forging something of a relationship with my mother.

Both hips have been replaced, but it's the left one that troubles her. In the short while that she's been here, hardly a couple of months, I've taken her to the doctor three times, and I am taking her there again, today, for another cortisone shot. Hopefully it will relieve some of the pain and stiffness. When I come to pick her up, she is already waiting for me at the front door of her apartment. She has on one of her favorite dresses, a black and white ensemble, and her face is made up with lipstick and the heavy rouge that many older women like to wear. Surely she's been preparing for hours, as she might for a date. It makes me think: this mundane experience of visiting a doctor is by no means mundane to someone whose health is faltering, who lives alone and seldom gets out. I should also mention that she is wearing heels, heels I believe may one day be the death of her.

"Mom," I say, "I wish you'd wear flats."

"I like my heels," she says. "I've worn heels all my life."

It's about pride. I understand this. It's about refusing to accept the rapidly narrowing boundaries of her life, and I respect this as well, but with two artificial hips she doesn't so much walk as teeter. I trail closely behind her as we make our way along the path to the carports, ready to catch her if she stumbles, afraid that each step might be her last.

I recently traded in my old BMW for a truck, and because it rides higher than most cars, it is difficult for my mother to pull herself up and into the passenger seat. To make her life easier, I built a strong wooden box for her to use as a step, and while I'm getting this box out from the bed of the truck, after I set it on the ground and unlock the door, I turn around and she is gone. I look down the path we just walked. She's not there. I look in the opposite direction. Nothing, no one. Then, out of sheer luck, I spot her just as she's turning the corner at the end of the carports.

She doesn't hear me.

"Mom," I call out again, louder, as I begin to run.

She's gone from sight now, heading where I have absolutely no idea, but I catch up with her a few seconds later.

I'm out of breath. I touch her arm to get her attention. She turns and looks at me. She studies my face, and for a moment she doesn't quite recognize me. Slowly, though, it dawns on her.

"Where'd you go?" she says.

"I didn't go anywhere."

"Don't leave me like that," she says.

* * *

The pain-relieving effects of cortisone are short lived.

The shots also don't always work, and apparently that's the case with my mother. The pain persists. The stiffness gets worse. Walking even a short distance winds her, and in the few weeks since her last doctor's visit she's developed a limp.

Certainly I want her to get better.

Certainly I don't want her to live in pain, and it wouldn't be so bad, having to shuttle her back and forth to the doctor, having to do her grocery shopping and banking, if I didn't sometimes feel that by helping her I'm betraying the memory of my family.

For the longest time, as a child, I denounced her for forging my father's name on the deed of trust to our house and selling it out from underneath us to cover her bad debts. For the longest time, as a child, I denounced her for constantly belittling my brother and sister, for telling them that nothing they did was good enough, for striking them too hard, too often. I denounced her for burning down an apartment building, an act that led to her incarceration; and when she was released two years later, I denounced her for taking us children from the father we loved and moving to L.A. But most of all, I came to blame her for the suicide of my alcoholic brother, a blame that lasted far beyond childhood, and one that may well have continued if I hadn't eventually come to understand better my own alcoholism. The root causes of addiction share linkage with the past, but in the end no one but the alcoholic is responsible for their destruction. This I learn through experience. We are in my truck now, headed for my mother's two o'clock doctor appointment, a follow-up for the ineffective cortisone shot. As we drive I glance over at her, and it strikes me, how as death nears the aged diminish, the body drawing into itself, the limbs thinning to little more than skin and bone. Time has rendered her once quick, violent hands powerless.

"I just want to thank you," she says.

"For what?"

"For taking me around all the time. I don't know what I'd do without you."

I appreciate her words. It is this arrangement, with me caring for her, or else a convalescent home, and she's not ready for that. I'm not ready to ask it of her, either, though I know the day may come when her life drains too much from my own, when she can no longer do even the smallest things for herself. Frail and weak, her beauty long faded, she is harmless now, this woman whom my brother, sister, and I feared, loved, and hated. As she stares straight ahead, her delicate fingers laced together and folded neatly in her lap, I glimpse the child in my mother, the tiny frame, the fragile skull of the very young, looking impossibly innocent, impossibly blameless.

* * *

This time the doctor recommends X-rays, speculating that maybe the steel rod in my mother's left thigh has somehow come loose. If so, it could be the cause of her suffering, and in the meantime, until he has these X-rays, he writes her a prescription for Feldene, a mild analgesic similar to aspirin. A few days later I drive my mother to the Palm Imaging Institute on 21st Street, directly across from Saint Bernardine's Medical Center where my ex-wife, Heidi, died soon after giving birth to another man's child. Being near this place sets off a wave of hard memories, and I suddenly feel the thirst for a drink, a tightening in the back of my throat. I get out of the truck. I go around to my mother's side and help her do the same. She's heard me talk about this hospital.

"That's where she died, isn't it?"

"Yes."

"Your brother," she says. "Your sister. Your dad, and now Heidi. You've lost too many."

In the radiology room, my mother lies on a stainless steel table. It is dark in here, just a dim light in one corner, and the machinery is large and old, painted gun-metal gray. The X-ray device slides along two heavy iron rods bolted to the ceiling above her, and as she rests there, her left hip positioned toward the lens, I think about her words. I think about how I can't go there, to the past and the places it takes me, because it takes me too far, and I need to remember the present. I need to remember I have three sons who need me here, who need me now. I need to remember that my second wife has come forward with her own love for my children, and that this love is strong and genuine, and that they are fortunate to have her, as I am. I need also to realize that I can't fully love and appreciate this woman, the way she deserves to be loved and appreciated, if I'm obsessed with the past. I am wasting her life by residing in another. It's about balance. It's about loving the living and missing the dead and I have never been able to clearly separate the two.

The radiologist motions for me to step behind the safety partition. Through a pane of thick glass I watch my mother, wondering why she and I are still here and the others are not, if it's about fate or chance, if it's purposeless or somehow by design. The radiologist presses a switch and a collision of atoms blast through my mother's body, bone, flesh, and skin.

* * *

My mother is returning from an afternoon bingo game at the recreation center when she takes a spill into a flower bed. This happens between doctor visits, before we get the results of her recent X-rays, and I don't know if the fall has anything to do with her wearing heels or not. Fortunately, though, the soil is moist and soft and serves to break her fall. A passerby helps her to her feet and escorts her back to the apartment where she phones me just as I'm sitting down to dinner with my wife and sons.

"Jimmy," she says, "I need you to drive me to the hospital."

"What happened?"

She tells me, and I shake my head.

"Did you break anything?"

"I hope not," she says. "But you should see my arm, it's completely black-and-blue."

"Can you move it?"

"It hurts when I do."

"But you can move it. That's a good sign," I say. "Hang on, I'm on my way."

The closest hospital is Saint Bernardine's, but I have no confidence in their doctors or staff. So I take my mother to a much better hospital in the neighboring city of Loma Linda, and on the way there she thanks me again. For driving her to the hospital. For, in general, looking after her. "I don't know what I'd do without you," she says, as she often does now, and that thought apparently triggers another, one about my brother and sister. "It'd be so much easier if Barry and Marilyn were alive. I'm sorry," she says, "that you have to do all this alone." I tell her it's not a problem. I tell her I want to help, and for a while she's quiet. For a while she just sits there holding her injured arm. "I don't know why they did it," she says. "Barry was doing so good as an actor. It's what he always wanted and he went so far, so quickly. I don't understand. And Marilyn, poor Marilyn, she was such a sweet girl. I don't know what got into her."

At one time, her words would've set me off. At one time, I would've told her that she was in many ways responsible for their suicides. I would've wanted her to admit guilt. I would've wanted her to acknowledge the lack of guidance she provided. I would've wanted to acknowledge my part in it all as well, if there was anything I could've done to save them and did not. But as the years have passed, and continue to pass, I have come to realize the worthlessness of guilt and blame and how hurt only begets more hurt.

"You holding up all right?" I ask.

"It aches bad."

"We're almost there," I say. "I'm sure they'll give you some pain medication.

At the emergency room, we're assigned a number and asked to wait. It proves a long wait, too, because the place is packed with the sick and injured, mostly the poor and undocumented. Finally, six hours later, we're called in. By this time the bruise has spread from just above her wrist to just below her shoulder, and it's darkened in color, a deep purple. I worry that she may have seriously hurt herself. I worry that her bones may have shattered. But when the results of her X-rays come back, the doctor tells us that it's only a hairline fracture to the upper portion of her arm. It will heal on its own. The severe bruising, he says, is common, particularly to the elderly. Oddly this good news seems to disappoint my mother, hungry for attention, any attention, and as we're leaving she whispers in my ear.

"He can't be right," she says. "We need to get another opinion."

But I don't want to think about any more doctors or X-rays, at least not now, not for a while, because I'm tired. I'm worn out. I drop my mother off at her apartment. I help her inside, and on the drive home, along a narrow highway that winds up into the San Bernardino Mountains, an old memory resurfaces: We are in our bedroom, my brother Barry and I, he is twelve and I am six, and she is beating him about the back with a bamboo spear we bought at Disneyland. The tip is made of rubber but the bamboo is real enough, and she strikes him repeatedly, until he's cowering in the corner. All I do is watch. As the youngest I escape the beatings my sister and brother endure, but later when she leaves, when Barry takes off his shirt, I will remember the many welts and the crisscross patterns they make across his back, already darkening, a deep purple, like the colors of the bruise spreading along our mother's arm.

* * *

The X-rays are in. These are the ones of her left hip, and once again I am driving my mother to the doctor's office. I am hoping the X-rays will reveal nothing out of the ordinary. I am hoping this appointment is not the precursor to an operation and that the doctor has discovered another, less serious cause for her pain. Going under the knife at her age can easily lead to infection, and infection for the elderly is often a death sentence. Ideally what ails her is something that can be managed with a pill, or physical therapy, and luckily this appears to be the case.

"Your X-rays look fine," the doctor says. "No breaks to the hip. The rod is aligned. I think you may have arthritis, which is not so bad. We can treat that. I'll write you a prescription for the pain and stiffness and I'd like to see you back here in a couple of weeks. Now," he says, "let's take a look at that arm."

Again, just as it happened in the ER, my mother seems oddly dissatisfied with the doctor's diagnosis. I am guessing here, but I imagine that she'd anticipated the worst, and instead of being relieved by the better news, she somehow feels jilted. How can the cause not be more serious? She doesn't see herself as a complainer, and neither do I, but I'm glad she won't have to risk another operation. The visit ends with the doctor recommending yet another set of X-rays, these for the injured arm, just to be sure it's healing correctly.

Back at her apartment, I fix us both a vodka tonic. After six months of abstinence, I am drinking again. I have been drinking off and on for the last several weeks, and trying, as I have often done in the past and failed, to limit myself to just a few, and only when the day is over, only when my work is done. I make mine strong, nearly straight up, and I make my mother's weak, so she won't get woozy when she stands up after I've left. She relaxes in the leather La-Z-Boy that I bought her, and I sit across from her on the couch.

Of course she knows about my problem, but she has no say over what I do, and besides, she likes a drink now and then herself. It loosens the tongue. It allows us to talk freely where we might ordinarily freeze up. Still, as I hand her her drink, she feels inclined to at least warn me.

"Be careful," she says. "Remember what happened to your sister and brother. I couldn't bear to lose my last child."

"Don't worry," I say. "I'm fine. I have it under control."

This is my mantra when I'm drinking, or about to take a drink, and I believe my words. The alcoholic mind is stunningly deceptive, but still there remains something inside me, a second voice, telling me that I am lying to myself. I ignore it. On the coffee table, I notice a framed snapshot of my mother and her husband, not my father but her second husband, posing on the sands in Hawaii, his arm draped across her shoulders, both wearing leis and smiling into the camera. She sees me staring at it.

"He was a good man," she says. "Not to slight your father, but Bud always did those little things. Flowers or perfume when I wasn't expecting it. You know we went to Hawaii not once but three times. I can't say your dad ever took me on a real vacation."

She fails to mention that she bankrupted my father. She fails to mention that she bankrupted her second husband not once but three times in the twenty-five years they were married and that these trips to Hawaii were made before and between those bankruptcies.

"That's nice," I say, and for the most part I mean it.

Because they look happy in the picture. And it would be wrong of me, I think, to begrudge anyone what little happiness they can take from this life, whether I believe they deserve it or not.

"He went so fast. He just kissed me goodnight and we fell asleep and when I woke up he was cold. His skin was blue." She takes a sip of her drink and sets it back down. "It's hard," she says, "living alone after all those years. I appreciate your staying and visiting for a while. I know you're busy. I know you have a family." She pauses. "It's strange, awful even, how quickly it goes. I hope there's an afterlife, but I really don't believe in it."

I fix us another drink.

I stay for a while longer and then I tell her I need to leave, that my wife is teaching a night class and it's my turn to make dinner for the boys.

At my house, I head upstairs to the bedroom to change into some sweatpants and a T-shirt, and as I'm doing this I look at another picture, one on my dresser, a framed black-and-white photograph of my mother and father taken shortly after they married. I pick it up. I hold it toward the light. In this picture my mother is thirty. My father, beginning to bald, is forty-four. They make a handsome pair with his sharp jawline, blue-gray eyes and fair skin, and my mother's olive complexion, her dark Sicilian eyes, and thick black hair. In her day she was a striking woman, and I wonder if this, her beauty, has anything to do with it, if it somehow predisposed her to expect more from life than life was willing to give.

I don't know.

I don't know a lot of things about my mother. I don't know a lot of things about my father, either, or of the other photos I find after his funeral, in the bottom of a box, faded snap-shots of Barry and Marilyn and myself, just a baby, when for a short while we resembled something of a family.

* * *

At this point, I lose count of the X-rays and doctor appointments. I resign myself once again to another visit to the Palm Imaging Institute for the hairline fracture to her arm and then, of course, the follow-up with the doctor to make sure that arm is healing correctly. They've become a nuisance, these trips, and I'm losing more time now than I'm willing to forsake. But I also realize that she's my duty, my care, and my responsibility.

At the age of fourteen I leave her, my brother, and my sister in Los Angeles and return to my father in San Jose, nearly four hundred miles across the state. I don't know how it is that my mother and I first give up on each other, who doesn't return the other's calls, or letters, if it's me, the irresponsible teenager, or her, the negligent parent. Who misses whose birthday? Who forgets to send a Christmas card, let alone a present? Although this sort of carelessness contributes to our estrangement, it is Barry's suicide that drives us furthest apart, accounting for our nearly twenty years of relative silence. And ironically it is suicide again, this time my sister's, that brings us back together. We are the sole survivors of a family that seems almost fated to self-destruct, and time for us is running out.

I pick her up a full hour early.

The Palm Imaging Institute isn't more than a few miles away, and I've arrived in plenty of time, but my mother feels otherwise.

"What took you so long?" she says. "Now we have to rush."

I don't argue. I don't see the point. In my truck, she informs me that we also need to do her grocery shopping after the X-rays, that she needs stamps, too, which means a trip to the post office, and since the bank is right next door she'd like to drop in there as well. Her dry cleaning, she says, can wait until next week, though she brings it with her in a brown paper bag "just in case it's not too much trouble to swing by the cleaners on the way back."

I take a deep breath.

The day will be longer than I expected, and here is how I see it unfolding: There will be more X-rays, if not for this injury then another. There will be more doctor visits, too, more prescriptions to fill, and I don't suppose, no matter what I tell myself, or how hard I might try, that my mother and I will ever be very close. As a parent myself, I can imagine nothing more devastating than losing a child to suicide, and for my mother there can be no abdication, no resolution, no peace. This is something we will both take to the grave, as my father does for his oldest son, never understanding, never reconciling, and it is good that he at least dies before his daughter. I don't suppose I'll ever entirely forgive my mother just as I am certain there are those who will never entirely forgive me. In this way we are the same, joined by blood and duplicity. We have ruined marriages, mine through drinking and using, hers over the compulsion for money, and our separate paths both leave behind a long line of wounded. We are the last of a troubled family, and when our day comes, I pray the legacy ends with us.

INSTRUCTIONS ON THE
USE OF ALCOHOL

I

You're young, maybe nine or ten, and your parents are throwing a party. All the adults are laughing and talking too loudly, in general having a good time, and you put two and two together. What makes them happy comes out of those bottles on the kitchen counter.

The brown ones, you learn soon enough, contain whiskey and scotch. The clear ones hold vodka and gin and that odd shaped bottle with the long neck, something called Midori, contains a thick syrupy green liquid. That's the one that intrigues you most, and when the adults aren't looking you pour yourself a glass. You sneak it into your room. You lock the door. At first you sniff at it, the green liquid, and because it doesn't smell so good you pinch your nostrils shut before you take a swallow.

It burns the back of your throat. It makes your eyes water. You shake your head, and for a few minutes, until the alcohol takes effect, you can't understand how anyone in their right mind could drink this stuff. But then a tingling sensation begins to spread through your chest, your face is warm and flushed, and you're suddenly light-headed. You feel good. In fact, you feel great, and now you understand why it's worth braving the foul taste, the burn in your throat, and the watery eyes. It's as if you've made a major discovery, a real inroad to the secret of a good life, and it only makes sense that if one drink has this effect on you that a second will make you feel even better. You finish the glass and sneak another. You repeat this action several more times.

The party ends around midnight, but you wouldn't know it because you're deathly ill. Because you've lost all that sugary green liqueur along with dinner and hors d'oeuvres before you promptly passed out in bed. In the morning, you wake with a miserable headache. Your mouth is so dry you can hardly swallow, you're still nauseous, too, and right then and there you swear never again to so much as look at a bottle of Midori. But what the seasoned drunk knows that the apprentice does not is that those of us predisposed to alcoholism are hardwired to quickly forget our unfortunate drinking experiences. In a day or two, all you remember is how good the liquor made you feel. So when you go over to a relative's house for dinner that following weekend, you find yourself sneaking into the kitchen again. You open the cupboard with the colorful bottles, and instead of the green stuff, because there is no green stuff in this household, you choose the liquid in the clear bottle with the Russian name of Stolichnaya. This brand burns more than the Midori but it also packs a faster, more effective punch, and that's exactly what you're after. Drunk, you find yourself smarter and funnier and stronger and braver and even better looking. For the budding alcoholic, booze seems to do more for you than it does for others, and your only regret, at least to date, is that you didn't come across this miracle potion sooner.

II

You're older now, maybe fifteen or sixteen, and by no stretch of the word would anyone outside of an uptight substance abuse counselor consider you a problem drinker, let alone an alcoholic. Liquor has actually lost some of its initial luster, and you rarely sneak drinks anymore, say, only once or twice a week. What currently interests you is marijuana and the intrigue that surrounds it. Booze just isn't as cool, and besides, you like the subterfuge, the cloak-and-dagger melodrama of doing something forbidden. Breaking the law is a high in itself and, just as importantly, it befits the rebel image of your teenage years. You enjoy scoring the weed behind the bleachers at James Lick High School almost as much as you do smoking it. You enjoy showing off to your friends how well you can roll a joint, and because the dope world has its own language, all the slang and clever code words, you feel special when you speak it. Tough. Street wise. And you don't for a minute believe all those lies you hear about marijuana being addicting. About how it damages the brain. If you want proof, just ask someone who's been smoking it daily for twenty years, but ask him slowly.

Then one day you try to connect with that kid behind the bleachers, the guy with all the Bob Marley stickers on his notebook, and it isn't happening.

"It's bone-dry out there," he says. "Fucking drought season, man."

Apparently some big bust went down in Humboldt County where they grow some of the world's best sensimilla, and now everyone's hoarding what they have and scrambling to find more. But he does have something else, if you're interested, this stuff he calls blow, a white powder you put up your nose. "It's good shit," he tells you. "Eighty percent pure." Since you've been such a loyal customer, he's willing to cut you a deal: a gram for fifty bucks, or an eight ball, three-and-a-half grams, for a hundred and twenty. It's too good to pass up, especially since there's no weed around, and there's also a party this weekend where you'd look pretty cool laying out some lines of coke in the bathroom for a few select friends. Or that girl you like. With some good dope and a little luck, you might even get laid. Blow, you've been told, is something of an aphrodisiac.

You enjoy making the buy, even more so now, because the stakes are higher with narcotics, the penalties worse if you're caught. You enjoy the preparations, carefully chopping the crystals with a shiny razor blade, drawing out neat even lines and scraping the bag, or bindle, for every last particle. And as it happens with your first drink, so it is with the coke. It makes you feel great. It makes you stronger and smarter and braver and even better looking. All your fears and insecurities fall to the wayside when you're wired, and you dismiss those lies you've heard about coke being addicting. Getting hooked is for weaklings, the idiots who can't control themselves, those losers who end up broke and penniless, wandering the streets at night like zombies, like the walking dead. You'll never be one of them, though you can see how the stuff might drain your bank account, since the rush is so short, and the more you use, the more it takes to get the same high. Where a couple of grams used to last you a week, now you're lucky if you can stretch that amount a full day. For the budding addict, the supply is never enough, but your only regret, at least to date, is that you didn't come across this miracle potion sooner.

III

You survive your teenage years. You even make it through college, drinking and drugging whenever you get a chance, which is about every other night, with all stops pulled out on the weekends. At this point, you're in your late twenties and still have no idea that you might have a slight problem. Who, after all, doesn't like to party? Who, after all, doesn't deserve a couple of drinks at the end of a hard day? A joint now and then never killed anybody, either. The same goes for a few lines of coke, a hit of Ecstasy now and then, or LSD, and a little heroin is actually a good thing if you're strung out on speed and need to settle your nerves.

Imagine how boring life would be if you had to live it straight twenty-four seven. Imagine how boring you'd be as a person if you couldn't get a little loose, a little crazy from time to time. The whole idea is to escape our dull existence, to find some amusement, some relief from the monotony of the day-to-day grind. This is how you rationalize it, anyway, and through the years you become very good at it. If you have a rough day, it's reason to drink. If you had a good one, it's reason to celebrate. And if you get into it with your wife, because somewhere in this chemical fog you fall in love and marry, that is definitely grounds for storming out of the house and holing up in the neighborhood bar. Lately this is the only place you seem to find any real peace, among men and women like yourself, the ones who don't judge you. So what if you like to drink yourself into a stupor. So what if you have a DUI or two. Half the people in this bar do, and like you they all chalk it up to the same thing: bad luck. Being in the wrong place at the wrong time. You actually drive better now after a couple of drinks, because you're safer, you take less chances, because you don't want to get busted again. And furthermore, if anyone's complaining, your drinking hasn't caused you to miss a day of work in months. That you're so hungover or strung out and frequently have to go home after lunch doesn't count.

You just can't understand why your wife continues to nag or break down in tears. All the bills are paid. The kids are clothed and fed and you and she both drive newer cars. For a drunk, you think, for a junkie, none of this would be possible. You'd have already lost it all or never made it to begin with. But whether you know it or not, and you don't know it yet, things are changing deep inside you and have been for some time: hormones, genes, brain chemistry, all of it adapts to the alcohol and drugs you continually dump into your body. The cells habituate. The cells literally mutate to accommodate your cravings and now they crave, too. Now your addiction has more to do with physiology than psychology. Now it's the body that robs the mind of its power to choose, and it's not long before you'll wish you never came across that miracle potion, those powders and pills.

IV

Add a few years to this story and you're in your thirties, still going strong. God knows what happened to your old college buddies who used to match you shot for shot, line for line. They can't keep up with you anymore and not a single one even wants to try. How they just turned their back on you and the partying life, simply because they landed good jobs and married and had kids, you can't understand. What you think has been your dirty little secret for years has in fact been no secret at all to anyone who's ever made the mistake of loving or caring about you.

"It's time to grow up," one says, when you call him late at night, drunk out of your mind.

Grow up, you think. Sure. Your friends have sold out to the doldrums of suburban middle-age. The truth is, you are and always have been tougher than them, blessed from the beginning with an iron constitution. A special ability to tolerate alcohol and whatever other poisons you consume. What you don't realize, however, is that this high tolerance is no gift but a liability, another sign and symptom of your addiction. And oddly enough, as you continue along this ever narrowing path, your tolerance will work exactly in the reverse, at least for the alcohol: where before it took ten drinks to get you reasonably drunk, now five will have you stumbling.

If you're not quite to this point yet, you're close. Your liver is enlarged. Your doctor has warned you, as has your boss, for all the days of work you've been missing lately, assuming she hasn't already fired you. Your marriage is in ruins, and you're up to your neck in debt. It makes you cringe to think of the thousands of dollars you've put up your nose or slapped down on the bar. The shame and guilt just compels you to drink more, and to start earlier, sometimes first thing in the morning, if only to quell the horrible hangover from imbibing too heavily the night before.

Hair of the dog.

That's the cure, and since you're always worn out, since you're not getting any younger, you need a little bump—compliments of methamphetamine—to get you through the long, hard day. Crank is cheaper than blow. It better fits your budget. Crank is also stronger, seven times stronger on the central nervous system, and at night you absolutely have to drink if you hope to sleep at all. At this stage of your addiction, your drinking and using has little to do with pleasure, or even escape. From here on out, it's about maintenance. From here on out, it's about feeding those mutated cells, fighting off the intense depression that follows a binge, and trying, to the best of your weakened abilities, to carry on the bare semblance of a life. You are teetering on the edge of becoming the very thing you most feared, another loser, another zombie, one of the walking dead who wander the streets late at night, nameless, lost, and forgotten.

V

Believe it or not, you hobble along like this for a couple more years. Obviously you've lost your job by now, or more likely several jobs, and your wife has left you and taken the kids. You're at a cold, ugly place in your life, and there doesn't appear to be any way out, any hope or chance of going anywhere but down. Then something happens. It could be a number of things. A close brush with death. A tragedy in the family, say, another DUI, a car wreck, or just a realization one morning when you look in the mirror and barely recognize the face before you. Somewhere in this haze, between sobering up and getting wasted again, it finally dawns on you that maybe, just maybe, you might have a problem.

These moments, however, are fleeting, especially when you try to quit, and you'll try many times in the next several months, only to find that by noon your hands are shaking so badly you can't hold a pen to sign your own name. Nausea quickly sets it, you sweat profusely, your head throbs, and you think to yourself: What the fuck am I doing? Give me a drink. A line. A pill. Anything to stop the pain. The cure is worse than the illness, and you're far less sick when you're drinking and using than when you attempt to stop. Inside of a day you're back at square one, and you hate yourself, as you lift the bottle to your lips, as you split open the bindle of coke or crank or whatever you could get your hands on. You hate yourself because you made a promise not to drink or drug for the day, and here you are, loaded again.

You're weak.

You're pathetic.

You consider killing yourself, since that's what you're doing anyway, albeit slowly, and you probably would if you didn't have kids. If you'd lost entirely your ability to love. Sometimes that's the only difference between life and death, and it surprises you, it takes you completely off guard that anyone in your family, that any of your old friends, still actually care about you. How is it that they see something in you that you can't see in yourself, something worth salvaging, when for the most part you've caused them nothing but disappointment, hurt, and shame. But they do, and one day when you come home to your crummy little apartment, or motel room if you've sunk that far, and find a half dozen friends and family waiting for you, the same ones who wouldn't return your late night calls because they knew you'd only phoned to ask for money.

"You're sick," they tell you. "You need help. This is something you can't do alone."

In a matter of minutes you're in the backseat of a relative's car, being kidnapped really, whisked away to a hospital for junkies and drunks where you remain for the next twenty-eight days.

That first week they keep you pretty anesthetized. To combat the onset of delirium tremens, the nurses give you round-the-clock doses of Valium, and because your blood pressure has rocketed off the charts you're also administered Clonidine, a powerful antihypertensive, to further reduce the possibility of stroke. For the harder cases, detoxing from drugs and alcohol without medical supervision can and occasionally does kill. Fortunately this is not your case, and just days after you've weathered the worst of it, you wake up one morning actually feeling rested, actually sober for the first time in you don't know how many years, and it occurs to you right then and there that you might have a chance. That there is at least hope, even for a sorry bastard like yourself.

VI

You're pushing forty now, a little beaten up for all the years of abuse, but for the most part you're still mentally and physically intact. You have no right to whine. No right to bitch. It's a minor miracle you're alive at all, and after a year or so of sobriety you start to get back some of the things you lost. Maybe it's your job, if you have an understanding boss. Maybe it's visitation rights with your kids, if only for every other weekend. But don't count on patching it up with your wife. She's already moved on to another man, the guy who consoled her while you were out partying. The house, too, she's keeping that and everything in it. You feel so much guilt for destroying your marriage that you don't dare fight for what's yours.

Where every night you used to get whacked out of your head, now you attend A.A. meetings. You arrive early and make the coffee. You set out the donuts and fold-out chairs, and when things are underway and you're called on to speak, when you're asked to "share," you follow the A.A. protocol and first announce yourself as an alcoholic and addict. This is an important tenet of your sobriety: to remember always and forever that you are marked, that there is no cure for your affliction. One drink triggers the craving, and once the craving is on you're off and running–next stop the dope man's house. Beating the physical part of addiction is a cakewalk compared to silencing that voice in your head, the one that never goes away, telling you it's okay to have a drink, a line, or a pill, because you've been clean and sober for a while. Because you can control it now. Compulsion is your soul mate, till death do you part, and your hold on sobriety is never more than tenuous.

But cheer up.

You've lost a lot but you've gained, too. If not wisdom, at least the return of your self-esteem. Your self-respect. And even though you've been condemned to a life sentence of A.A. meetings, even though you'll always wrestle with your addiction and may wind up back in rehab, at least for now, if only for this day, you are free of the miracle potions, powders, and pills. If only for this day, you are not among the walking dead.

REMEMBERING LINDA

Late at night, Linda slips out of her bedroom window. She moves quietly across the backyard. She opens the gate and just as quietly closes it behind her. A lowered Chevy Impala is parked at the curb with its headlamps turned off. When the door opens, the cab light comes on, and I see him, the man behind the wheel. He's too old for her, in his early twenties probably, and he has a ponytail, the hair pulled back tight across his skull. Linda wears a high school varsity jacket and tight Levis that show off the smooth, rounded curves of her hips. She slips into the car and they kiss. A light rain has begun to fall. I am watching this scene, as I have twice before, through the broken slat in the blinds covering my window.

At breakfast the next morning, all is as usual. Linda is dressed in the uniform required of the students at Saint Francis: a plaid skirt with a white cotton blouse, black leather shoes, and white socks that reach to the knee. She sits across from Helen, who wears the same. They're both seventeen but Helen is the quiet one, in part, I think, because her teeth have grown in badly. The top incisors project at odd angles, forcing the others into a crooked row so that whenever she smiles or laughs, which is not often, she hurriedly covers her mouth with her hand. She is a small girl, barely five-feet, her skin is dark, and her hair is thick and coarse.

Aileen is the woman who owns this house, and this morning she serves up plates of bacon, scrambled eggs, tortillas, a small bowl of salsa, and a bottle of ketchup for my father because he doesn't much like salsa. He sits at the head of the table, his face hidden behind the morning paper. Aileen only accepts female foster kids, for the boys, she says, can be dangerous, and she has no time for the girls who don't mind her. There are too many others willing and waiting to take their place. She pauses over Linda as she sets a glass of milk in front of her.

"You look tired," she says.

"I was up late."

"How come?"

"Homework," Linda says. "Tons of algebra."

"Maybe you should get started a little earlier."

"I will."

"I hope you're not wasting your time. You know the rules.

No boyfriends. No dating. Your job is to get good grades in school, and my job is to make sure you do."

"I understand."

"Just keep your nose to the grindstone like Helen, and you'll be just fine here."

Linda's face reddens, from embarrassment or anger, I can't tell. Helen is quiet and seems distant. But she hears everything, and I sense it, that she's somehow pleased.

I attend Fredrick Martin Middle School, but it's on the way to Saint Francis, and the best part of my day is walking there with Linda. Helen comes with us, though she usually trails a few steps ahead or behind, and she rarely contributes to the conversation. I don't say much, either, but that's only because I have to be on top of things. We live in a bad neighborhood in East San Jose where people install bars over their windows and doors, where teenagers hang out on the corners, drink and smoke dope, and where at night you sometimes hear gunfire. I am Linda's protector. I am here to defend her honor. To take on all comers regardless of age or size. I am fearless. I am tough, and as we walk I keep my hand in my pocket, rubbing my thumb along the pearl-white casing of my jackknife.

But it's hard not to drift, and occasionally I forget my role as bodyguard and slip into another imaginary world. This one belongs to Linda and Key West and Cancun and Jamaica and their beautiful sandy white beaches with clear blue water that is always warm. She says she's been to them all. Then there are the stories about her father and their old house in Santa Monica with floor-to-ceiling windows overlooking the Pacific.

"In the summer," she says, "we used to walk down to the pier and ride the roller coaster. Once my dad took me on it six times in a row. Can you believe that?" she says.

"Believe what?"

She lightly punches me in the arm.

"Six times in a row, man. Shit," she says, "were we dizzy."

I know she's lying. I lived in L.A. for seven years with my mother, brother, and sister, and I know for a fact that there is no roller coaster on the pier in Santa Monica because I've been there. It was torn down, I was told, back in the 30's. But Linda, like Helen, is a foster child from the County of Santa Clara, and I don't care if she lies because it's the lies that make her feel better about herself, and I believe Linda needs that. I need it for her, too, and it's why I listen. It's why I don't question or show doubt because most people who take in children from the county, Aileen included, really only do it for the money, and Linda knows it. So must Helen. They're not necessarily wanted, and maybe they never have been, not even by their own parents, assuming they ever knew them. Linda had been living here for about four months when my father and I came along. As for myself, I'd just left L.A. and moved in with my dad barely five months ago. For Helen, she'd been here four years.

"Next July, when I turn eighteen," Linda says, "I'm going back to Cancun. Of course I also want to go to college, so I'll probably only stay a year." She looks over her shoulder. Helen has fallen behind. Hey," she says, "hey, Helen, how about you? What do you want to do?"

Either she doesn't hear Linda or else she's ignoring her.

I don't know. In any event Helen doesn't answer. I take up the slack.

"She wants to be a nun," I say.

"Really?"

"I heard her and Aileen talking."

Being a nun is a serious vocation, requiring vows of poverty, chastity, and obedience, and for what seems a long while none of us say a word. Finally Linda breaks the silence.

"You know," she says, as if she's given the matter considerable thought. "That's a good thing. To serve our Lord. I know for an absolute fact you'll make a great nun."

Helen smiles, then she remembers her bad teeth, and quickly catches herself. By now we've reached the gates of Saint Francis, and after saying our goodbyes I continue on alone.

In school I find it impossible to concentrate. All I can think about is Linda. Linda Hernandez. I like how her last name rolls off the tip of my tongue, and I repeat it to myself, silently, several times. At fourteen I am caught in those most tender years of adolescence where even the smallest difference in age presents a vast, insurmountable divide for my love. But somehow, someway, I want to believe that she will in time come to realize the depth and intensity of my feelings for her. And in knowing this depth, in knowing that no man could ever possibly match such love, she will vow to wait for me. It will be hard at first, and for a while people will talk badly about us, especially against Linda, but we'll survive. In the end, we'll be stronger because of it.

I have other more intimate thoughts about Linda and what I'd like to do to her. Typically they come at night as I lay awake beside my father, too restless to sleep. We share a queen-sized bed in a room that was once a two-car garage, and though it's been nicely remodeled, it's still basically a cold, drafty garage with a window built on a concrete slab. This is winter time, and for a carpenter, when the weather turns bad and stays bad for very long, and when some of your customers are slow paying up, it's easy to find yourself in a fix. Our being here is only supposed to be temporary until we can get back on our feet, but there's more to it than that: Aileen and my father are a couple. They've been in love for years, even before they both divorced, and I can see how our present situation might easily become permanent. Meanwhile, they sleep in separate rooms, if only for appearance's sake—for Helen mostly, I suppose, and for Linda and the county social workers. I certainly hope they don't think they're doing it for me because I've already had the embarrassing misfortune of having walked in on them.

For now, however, they go about pretending.

For now, my father is asleep. For now, it's close to midnight when I hear the opening of her bedroom window again.

It's been two weeks since she last sneaked out to meet him, the guy in the lowered Chevy Impala, and any dreams I might've had of them breaking up are dashed. Slowly, quietly, so as not to wake my father, I climb out of bed and look through the broken slat in the blinds covering the window. It's the same scene, only tonight she wears a dress, and when the car door opens, as Linda slides across the seat and they kiss, I turn away.

She comes back about an hour later.

In the morning, when the house begins to stir, I hear her footsteps in the hallway outside my room. I hear the opening and closing of the bathroom door, the knocking of the pipes in the wall, and then the spray of water beating against the porcelain tiles of the shower stall. I imagine her holding her hand to the water, testing it, then letting her robe fall gently to the floor. I wait for the water to shut off. I wait for the sound of the door knob turning, and I time it so that we meet when she steps out of the bathroom. Her hair is wrapped in a blue towel, fashioned into a turban, and I like how our shoulders brush as we slip by each other in the hall. I like how she smiles, out of one corner of her mouth, and in passing I inhale deeply, taking in the scent of her freshly washed body.

"Good morning," she says.

"Morning," I say.

She smiles at me.

I look away. I look down at the floor.

"What's a matter?" she says.

"Nothing," I say.

It's only shyness, of course. I'm just a boy but it's the gesture, the simple gesture of looking away, as if in disgrace, that later would've led her to believe that I had informed on her when in fact nothing could've been further from the truth. I am guilty of a betrayal I never committed.

That morning she does not come to breakfast, and when I ask about her, Aileen tells me that Linda isn't feeling well. That she won't be going to school today. Helen and I walk the route without her, and I don't recall us talking, though I'm sure we exchanged goodbyes at the gates of Saint Francis. At this point, I have no reason to hate. The thing is, Linda isn't there when I get home from school, and on the way down the hall I pass her room. The door is open but the bed has been stripped to the mattress. All the small colorful bottles on top of her dresser are gone. The nightstand is also bare.

In the living room, I find Helen in the leather recliner, her feet curled beneath her, running her fingers through decade after decade of her rosary. "Where's Linda," I ask, but she doesn't answer. On her face I detect the faint hint of a smile,and suddenly I realize what she has done. I look away, as I did with Linda, only this time it is with disgust. At fourteen, my eyes burning, I don't fully understand the source of my contempt. I am blinded with fury. But in remembering Linda, decades later, my sight has cleared. I recognize the girl. I recognize both girls as only children, each abandoned, wanting only to love and be loved.

THE APPRENTICE

My father is spreading tar on the roof of a tract home during a rainstorm. He's sixty-seven years old. I'm seventeen. He's teaching me how to patch a leak. You have to isolate it first. You have to find the cracks, usually several feet above where the water drips through the ceiling in the house, and then you clean them. "Remove any loose gravel," he tells me, "scrape out any debris." We're thoroughly soaked, it's freezing cold and I'm shivering, but still I listen. Still I watch, paying close attention to how he smoothes the tar with a spatula, the same one we use for drywall, and then fans it out, above and below the cracks, as well as into them. In the distance, I hear the rumble of thunder, and for a moment the dark sky brightens with lightening.

I want to learn the trade.

My father is good at what he does. I want to know what he knows. I want the knowledge of a lifetime pounding nails, building and remodeling homes. Still, when more fortunate men are retired, he's patching leaks in the middle of a storm.

"Be generous with this stuff," he says. "Better more than too little."

It's the winter of 1973, and I'm in my senior year of high school. In a few months I have to make a decision about whether I should attend college or continue on with my father, learning the trades, from plumbing to carpentry. When I know enough, I could take over his small business and expand it, because I am young. Because I am strong and ambitious. Though I like to think I'm smart, I've never done well in school, struggling for C's and D's in every subject except English and P.E. My SAT scores are barely average, and I can't see myself spending another four or five years sitting in a cramped desk in a cramped classroom, listening to some burned-out teacher.

Another bolt of lightening brightens the sky. It strikes closer than the last, and the crack of thunder seems louder.

"Let's get off this roof," my father says. "We're done here."

He reaches for the bucket of tar, but I grab it first. It comes in a five-gallon can, like paint, and because it's heavy I prefer to carry it. My father climbs down the ladder and then steadies it for me. The rungs are wet and slick. With the rain in your eyes, and hauling this bucket, it would be easy to slip. It would be easy to fall, and it's a known fact that a young man heals better and faster than someone my father's age. This is another reason why I don't want to go to college. I'm scared that one day I won't be there and he'll lift something too heavy, lumber maybe, or drywall, and seriously damage his already injured back.

Or worse, he could have a heart attack.

He could have a stroke. Although my dad and Aileen are still together, in fact they're talking marriage, I worry that something bad might happen. I worry he'll need me, and where will I be, miles away, kicking back in some warm and cozy classroom talking about books and stories.

* * *

In school, I am listless. Except for my creative writing class with Mrs. Bettencourt, where I'm able to write whatever I please, I am bored. That I don't yet understand all the rules of grammar doesn't matter much to this teacher. Of course she circles my misspellings in red pen and corrects my most egregious errors, but she also makes all sorts of generous comments in the margins. On one page she might remark on how the dialogue sounds authentic. On another she may compliment me on the way I've described a young girl, say, or the light from a street lamp on a foggy night.

But Mrs. Bettencourt is only a substitute teacher, albeit a long-term one, and once, after class, she confides in me: Although it's been a dream of hers to become a teacher, the pay is awfully low, jobs are scarce, and at the end of the semester she is returning to her position as the manager of a bank. "Practical concerns," she says. "Sometimes you just have to get real." And those words stay with me, reinforcing what I already know to be true. Even my school counselor, back in my junior year, suggests I drop out of regular classes and attend the vocational center where I can learn a trade. My father, however, refuses to sign the release form, and when I press him he gets angry.

"How come?"

"Because I want you in school."

"But vocational school *is* school."

"No," he says. "No, not really. You tell that sonofabitch counselor I said to stick it where the sun don't shine."

I think my father is wrong.

I think, given my lousy grades, that he has to get real. At night, as the days toward summer drag on, I often find myself unable to sleep. We've moved out of Aileen's house and are on our own again, just me and my dad, and I feel a great, unyielding pressure. I have to make a hard decision, and it needs to be the right one, and I need to make it very soon. Part of me wants to please my father who dropped out in the eleventh grade to work and help his father. Part of me wants to break the cycle of the men in our family working the trades and be the first to attend college. My older brother did it his own way by becoming an actor, and a successful one, too, right out of high school. And I admire him for it. But I also need to realize that I'm not nearly as smart and set my sights accordingly.

I can pound a nail straight and true.

I can throw a roll of ninety-pound roofing over one shoulder and climb a twenty-foot ladder with it. I can carry two sheets of half-inch drywall by myself and tack them up in record time. These are talents as real as any, and I'm no fool. I know I have to focus. I know I have to play to my strengths and that means recognizing my limitations. That means conceding and setting my sights accordingly. And the sooner I accept it, the sooner I can get on with the business of life.

* * *

In May, when the weather is clear and warm, I help my father pour a concrete driveway. The old one is nothing more than gravel and potholes, and because the owner is getting ready to sell, retire, and move out of state, he wants to improve the property so that he can get top dollar. Ordinarily, my father doesn't do this sort of work, but the man is a friend, a mechanic by trade, and they've agreed to an even swap. We pour him a driveway, he rebuilds the engine of my father's truck, a beat-up old Chevy with over 170,000 miles on it. Dollar for dollar, the friend is getting the better deal, but this is typical of my father. He always gives the customer a break. He always bids too low, and we end up working for little more than time and material. There are occasions when we barely break even.

"We're lucky to have a job," he says. "I'm getting up there, you know, and in this business people don't want to hire an old man."

I don't like when he talks this way.

I don't like to think about him growing older, slowing down, and I especially resent the occasional client who appears to pity him. Because I'm there, too, his right-hand man. If there's heavy lifting, I can do it. He's the brains. I'm the muscle.

We make a good team, and when it comes to concrete, he definitely needs help. He builds and secures the forms while I'm in school, but I have to take off the next day. It's a tricky situation. Concrete is finicky, and we certainly wouldn't pour it in the winter with the threat of rain. On the other hand, if it's too hot out, it'll dry too quickly and crack. Ideally we pour in moderate temperatures, and that's what we do here. The cement truck arrives in the morning, dumps its load, and leaves us to the hard labor of spreading it out with shovels across the entire driveway. After that we use a tamper to sink the rocks. Then we have to smooth it all out with a spade, so there are no dips for water to collect. I could go on, but the point is this:

it's a back-breaking job, and we need to do it quickly and efficiently before the cement sets. If we don't, the whole thing is ruined.

So we work hard.

So we work fast, and by mid-afternoon we've knocked it out. But the hurried pace comes at a cost. We both end up unusually drained. The muscles in my shoulders and arms ache, and the lime from the cement, where it seeped through my gloves, has burned the softer skin on the back of my hands.

In the truck now, heading home, I look over at my father. He's beat too. I can tell by the red rings around his eyes and how his arms hang heavy on the steering wheel.

"How's your back," I say.

"A little sore," he says. "But it's okay."

In a couple of days I'll be fully recovered, even stronger for the experience, but it'll be a week or better for my father.

I've seen it before. He'll drink a little heavier. He'll sleep a little longer. He'll end the next few days a little earlier. But he knows what he can and cannot take, and it's not the child's place to admonish the parent. I'd like to think that if he had money enough he wouldn't be doing this anymore, only I know better. I know my father and, poor or not, he'll be hanging drywall, patching roofs, and pounding nails until he can no longer hold a hammer.

* * *

In the high school I attend, on the poor side of San Jose, most of us do not go on to college. It's largely a disadvantaged and minority population, and nearly half of us drop out before our junior year. Others stumble valiantly on to graduate, but few of us care to take our education further. I have classmates who boast that they've never read a book cover to cover.

Many of us go into the trades. Many of us start with low paying jobs and work our way up. In my circle of friends, I don't personally know of anyone who made it through junior college, let alone earned a bachelor's degree. Still others choose the dark path. I know of several former classmates who've done long stretches of hard time.

Blame it on the parents. Blame it on the environment, the system, the schools, or the teachers.

All I'm trying to say is that I'm not alone in my uncertainty. Like my friends and classmates, I have little faith in myself. Like my friends and classmates, I am troubled. I am confused, and in the days to come I look to my older brother for advice.

I write Barry a long letter confessing my dilemma, my ambivalence, and with it I enclose a short story I wrote in Mrs. Bettencourt's class. It's not the first time I've sent him my work. For years he's encouraged me to read and write, and I like to please him. This one is about the last day in the life of an eighty-seven year old man whose only real contact with the outside world is a monthly visit from the county social worker. I have him sitting in a rocking chair on the front porch of his rundown house. I have him drinking a glass of red wine. The whole story takes place in his head, and he dies quietly, as easily as closing his eyes, while he waits for the social worker to arrive.

My brother phones me about a week after I send the letter.

"College isn't for everybody," he says, "and there's nothing wrong with being a carpenter like Dad. Either way, it's a tough call, but whatever you do, I'd hate to see you quit writing. That story you sent me," he says, "it's really good."

* * *

My father and I are clearing a blocked sewer line. Over the last week, temperatures have reached record highs, and today promises to be no different. By ten in the morning it's already in the 80s, and I'm not halfway through the first part of the job. I'm sweating. Flies buzz around my head. Some even bite. This scene is set in the front yard of a house in Los Gatos, an upper middle class suburb of San Jose, and I am digging a hole in the lawn.

Typically, sewer lines are laid four feet beneath the ground. In older homes, this line is four inches in diameter and made of terra cotta. It comes in six foot lengths, each section joined at the flanged end and sealed with cement. But sometimes that seal cracks, it begins to leak, and if there are any trees in the near vicinity their roots, in search of water, will grow into the line and plug it up. That's the case here, and while my father is inside the house replacing the damaged floor in the bathroom, he puts me to work shoveling. We've already isolated the point of the blockage by running a plumber's snake through the line, marking where it hangs up, then pulling it out and measuring the length. Give or take a foot or two, it's a fair estimate. The ground, however, is full of rocks, and they make the digging hard, frustrating, and tedious. Every couple of minutes I'll hit a big one and have to stop, throw down the shovel, and shimmy it loose with a tire iron. Then, as the hole grows deeper, I have less room to maneuver, and I scrape my elbows against the sides. I scrape my knuckles, too, and my left shoulder. Finally, bruised and exhausted and a little bloody for it all, I uncover the sewer line. It has to be two, maybe three in the afternoon. The temperature is in the low hundreds, and the humidity makes it even worse.

I look up from the hole.

My father is standing above me. He hands me down a cold chisel and a ball-peen hammer.

"See that flange there?"

"Yeah," I say.

"An inch or so below it," he says. "I want you to chip me out a hole about the size of a Kennedy half-dollar."

I wipe the sweat from my brow with the back of my arm and set to work. Again it's a tedious process, though of a different sort. Instead of pure muscle and stamina, this requires a certain skill. If I'm careless, if I hit the chisel too hard, I could easily crack the entire pipe. So I have to work slowly, literally chipping away at it, a sliver at a time. My father tells me these things, calmly guiding my every move. He is a good, patient teacher.

What he does not tell me, however, is what to expect when I chip out the last sliver. In a matter of seconds, through that opening only the size of a Kennedy half-dollar, I am suddenly knee-deep in foul smelling shit and urine. Flecks of toilet paper float on the surface.

"Son of a bitch," I say.

Naturally, I gag.

Naturally, I try to scramble out of the hole, but I don't get far.

"Not so quick," my father says. He hands me a key-hole saw with its long, narrow blade meant for use in tight places. "Now I want you to reach on down there and cut out that root clogging the line. You want to learn the trades, plumbing's a part of it, and this is a part of plumbing. Let me know when you're done," he says. "I'm just about finished inside."

Reaching down there, all the way up to my shoulder in lukewarm shit, my face only inches away from it as I work, I'm astonished I don't lose my lunch. Afterwards, saturated from the neck down in sewage, my father has me stand in the middle of the lawn and sprays me off with the garden hose. A couple of teenagers watch from across the street. One is laughing.

On the ride home, I am angry. My back aches from the hard digging. I'm sopping wet. I literally stink like shit and all I want to do is get back to the house and take a long hot shower. Of course my father senses my anger and tries to make it good.

"For what it's worth," he says, "I'm paying you double-time today. How about we stop off somewhere and get a coke?"

But I don't answer him. I don't say a word, and when he reaches over to pat my shoulder, I pull away. Although I know it's not plausible, I feel as if he's set me up. The timing is just too perfect. Somehow he planned for this sewer to back up so that I could have the wonderful opportunity of unclogging it. At seventeen, I resent him for giving me the job, for tipping the scales toward college. At seventeen, I resent him for not warning me of what to expect, and it's only later, years later, that I understand how little it had to do with sewer lines and ditches.

I see us now.

I see the father, worn out from another hard day, his face slack with fatigue. I see the apprentice seated beside him in that old pick-up truck with the windows rolled down because of the smell. Because of the heat. The boy is sullen. The boy is angry. But in time, when he has his own sons and the father has passed on, he'll know the importance of believing in the child until the child learns to believe in himself.

THIS RIVER

This river is over 800 miles from my home in Southern California. This river is wide and passes through steep, deeply divided and lightly vegetated mountainous terrain. It is more than 55 miles long. At its mouth, this river is narrow and rocky, but further down it widens and the mountains give way to more densely forested hills. This river is pure and clean, and in it thrive steelhead, cutthroat and rainbow trout. But the Chinook salmon born to these same waters spend only a short part of their lives here. Then they migrate to the ocean where they will wander for years before attempting to return to their natal stream.

Some travel as far as 2,500 miles out to sea, and only a small percentage ever succeed in making the dangerous trip home. Many do not carry enough body fat and fail through starvation. More are caught in fishermen's nets. Otters, eagles and bears snatch others in the shallower waters. The stronger, fortunate females that survive the journey will lay eggs. The stronger, fortunate males spread the milt. Just days after spawning, giving life to the next generation, they all will then die.

I come here in the summer when the migration of the salmon is over and the rapids move more slowly. I come here with two of my sons, Logan and Nate, driving over ten hours to reach this place, this spot on the Chetco River in Oregon where, twelve years before, I spread the ashes of my father. In a few days, I will spread the ashes of my brother along these waters.

My little boy, Nate, only nine, finds the box of remains in the bed of my truck while we're setting up our camp site. It's wrapped in white paper with an envelope taped to one side.

"What's this?" he says.

I look over my shoulder. He holds the box up to his ear. He shakes it.

"Something's rattling."

"Those are bones," I say.

He makes a face.

"Yuck," he says, putting the box down.

"That's your Uncle Barry," Logan tells him, "the one dad's always talking about, the guy in the movies."

"Oh," he says. "Sorry."

"It's okay," I say. "There's nothing to be sorry about.

Just put the box up front under the seat."

I've shown them videos of *Bad Company* and *Daisy Miller*, both films in which my brother starred. The boys know what he looks like as a young man, forever young in celluloid, but they never met. They know only the characters he played, not the real Barry, the one who would've liked to hold them. To have fun with them. To be the good uncle, had he sobered up.

This trip to the Chetco is not a simple sojourn for the dead. It is instead, as it should be, about the living. It is, among the less tangible, about teaching my sons what my father taught me. How to pitch a tent. How to shoot a .22 rifle straight and true. How to string tackle and bait a hook and where to throw your line for your best chances of catching a fish.

Typically they feed in the early morning, just after sunrise, and as the day grows warmer they escape the summer heat by swimming deeper. On full bellies, they remain there, circling lazily until the evening, when it cools off and they rise again to snap up the gnats and mosquitoes that linger too long, too close to the surface of the water. In my mind I can see my father. I can hear his voice:

"They're in the deeper pockets," he says. "In the white water where it curls over the rocks. You fish downstream, not up. Trout are shy and smart." My father tosses the hook and sinker with ease and precision into a pocket of white water. The force of the current immediately draws the line taut.

"Remember, if you can see them, they can see you and won't bite." He squats on his haunches. I do the same and he hands me the pole. He is not smiling, at least not yet. For my father, fishing is something of an art born of necessity, an essential skill acquired to put food on the table, and he wants me to take this lesson seriously. "When you feel a nibble, give it a little tug. Tease it, and when it strikes hard pull up fast. That'll hook it."

I am serious.

My attention is sharp and focused because I'm intent on catching a fish and showing my father that I am capable of doing so. Quickly, with beginner's luck and good instruction, I snag what feels like a big one. The trout shoots out of the water.

"You got her," he says. "Just stay calm. Reel her in slow."

It's a fighter, squirming and flapping and twisting, even when I've worked it from the river and onto the sandy bank.

It's an easy nine or ten inches.

"A keeper," my dad says.

He pats me on the back. The smile so far denied me is now present on his face, and for this first catch he does the honors of dislodging the hook from its mouth. He helps me with my line and casting and baiting several more times before he leaves, so he can fish himself. My father is not a bait-and-hook man, but I'm only around Nate's age, nine or ten, and not yet ready for lessons in the higher art of fly fishing.

* * *

This is not your usual camp ground. There are no showers, no toilets or bathrooms. There are no picnic benches or barbecue pits. No motor homes. No trailers. Out here there is no loud music, no beer guzzling teenagers. Out here you are very much alone, and this, of course, is the way my sons and I like it. In the four nights we spend here, I think we see a total of three people. Maybe four.

During the day, the boys strip down to their swim trunks and play in the river. I watch them from a portable lounge chair, glancing up every now and then from the book I am reading. It's about a boy and his very odd and unfortunate upbringing with a disturbed mother. My own mother was similarly afflicted, her temper unpredictable, one minute enraged and striking out, the next sad and remorseful. Once, while we were driving on the Hollywood Freeway, she said something to Barry and he said something back. I don't remember what set her off, though it didn't typically take much, but nothing justified her suddenly speeding up and swerving from lane to lane, throwing us back and forth in our seats, screaming, "I'm going to kill us, I'm going to kill us all." Sometimes, after one of these episodes, she'd later shower Barry, Marilyn, and me with gifts bought of guilt: a guitar, an aquarium, a new pair of shoes. I look at my boys, knowing they too have suffered. For them it is the sudden and unnecessary death of their mother at the hands of incompetent doctors. For them it is my own struggle with mental illness, alcohol, and drugs. I would like to tell them that there will be no more slips, no backsliding, because that other father, the sick one, is gone forever. I would like to promise them the security and stability that all children deserve. But there are no guarantees for people like me, and I fear I will let them down again. No gifts will relieve the guilt of relapse. No gifts will soothe their pain, and I offer none, learning from my mother that you can't buy your way out of humiliation and shame.

Toward sunset, the boys and I gather the fishing gear and follow a narrow dirt road up and around the river, over a small bridge, and then down again to its banks. The evening is warm and the smell of the surrounding ferns and saplings is thick and sweet. Logan is old enough to rig his own line, but this is Nate's first time and he needs my help. I show him how to put on the small beaded weights. I show him how to tie the proper knots. I show him how to bait, and seeing his squeamish face, as I thread the nightcrawler through the hook, reminds me of my own reaction the first time my father showed me the same. All that ooze and guts. The squirming, agonizing pain of the worm as you impale it. I no more wanted to kill the poor thing than dirty my hands in the process. Again I hear my father's voice:

"Hold it like this and run it straight through. If you can see the hook, so can the fish, and they won't bite."

I cast the line out for Nate, as my father did for me the first time. It lands in white water curling over a rock.

I expect him to snag.

I expect him to lose his line often, as I did at his age, and so we'll fish together this camping trip, sharing the one pole.

"Keep your line taut," I say. "When you get a nibble, pull back just a little bit. Tease it, and when it bites hard, jerk up on it."

"What's a bite feel like?"

"You'll know when it happens."

He's wearing my Yankees baseball cap. Occasionally it lips down his forehead, covering his eyes, and he nudges it back up. I smile. He's a little guy, one of the smallest in his classes with brown hair and round eyes that remind me of his mother. For junior wrestling this year, he weighed in at a whopping fifty-two pounds. I notice the tip of his pole dip.

"That's a nibble," I say.

"Should I pull up?"

"When it strikes again," I say. "Be ready."

He crouches down.

"I'm ready," he says, and he says it very seriously. His eyes narrow. He stares intently at the tip of his pole, all focus and concentration, and sure enough, a few seconds later, when the fish strikes again, he pulls up and hooks it.

"I got it," he says. "I got it. I got it."

It's a classic moment for any father—watching your child excited, reeling in his first fish. Unfortunately this one is the size of a minnow, and while it's flipping around on the rocks, fighting to free itself, Logan feels compelled to point out the obvious. It is the job of all older brothers to squelch the joy of younger siblings, the quicker the better. My oldest son Andy, who could not make this trip, did the same to Logan, who is simply upholding tradition.

"Yeah," he says, "you caught a sardine."

"Shut up," Nate says.

"*You* shut up."

"At least I caught *something*."

I am, at this point, struggling to remove the hook from the fish's tiny mouth without killing it, and I don't need any distractions. In the minute this process takes, I've worked up a sweat, and it is with considerable relief that I toss the baby trout back into the river, only to watch it float belly up.

"Shit," I say.

"We should've kept it," Nate says.

"You wasted a life," Logan says.

"I didn't. Dad did."

The current catches the baby trout, pulls it under and away, so that soon it's out of sight, out of mind. But there are more where this came from, plenty more, and larger. Inside of an hour they've caught their limit and we're headed back to camp, all smiles, the boys eager for their first fresh trout dinner.

* * *

This is not at the Chetco River. This is in a run-down house my father rented after he got back on his feet, a few years after we moved out of Aileen's place. This is at the kitchen table. Today we finished roofing a home, it's evening, and we're drinking Pabst Blue Ribbon. My father is old school, believing if I'm man enough to put in a full day pounding nails and hanging shingles, I'm man enough to have a couple beers. I'm sixteen.

When he drinks, he likes to reminisce, and he often talks about the Chetco, the years of his youth spent there, camping and fishing and swimming. He talks of one day building a home along its banks to bring his children together. To surround himself with us. But his words are empty. He is a poor man after our mother bankrupts him, and too old by then, too worn out, to recover his losses. Still he talks.

I'm not sure what gets into me. I'm not even sure why the subject crosses my mind, but I'm light-headed with alcohol, and it's emboldened me. I'm young and my mouth works too easily. My father, however, is unfazed.

"Are you ever scared of dying?"

"What brought that up?"

I don't say anything.

He smiles at me and chuckles.

"Death is nothing to be afraid of."

He grew up around the Cherokee, and though baptized Methodist, he rarely spoke of Christ and didn't care for organized religion.

"What comes of the earth," he says, "returns to the earth. Your spirit goes into a pool of deep water where it mixes with the spirits of all God's creatures. The bear. The mountain lion. The squirrel. The deer. Who are we to think we're any better?" He puts his hand on top of mine resting on the table. He smiles again, knowing, I believe, that my question implies the child's fear of losing his parent. "There's nothing to worry about. The calm water feeds into the rapids and carries you on. The spirit never dies," he says, "it just follows the river."

A decade later, I'll return to the Chetco for my father. I bring Andy, my oldest at twelve, and Logan, just six. Nate has yet to be born. The lessons learned, on that first trip, run deeper than showing my sons how to pitch a tent, to shoot a rifle, to string tackle and bait a hook. It's the experience itself. It's the wedding of the past with the present, the time we spend together, and the time we'll never have again. It's about the loved and beloved and the memories that survive us.

* * *

This rifle is a Winchester .22 pump with a smooth wooden stock and bluing that has yet to wear. This rifle that my sons shoot in the evenings, before the sun sets, first belonged to my father. Then he passed it on to Barry, his oldest son, who eventually passed it down to me, and sometimes when I hold it, if only for a moment, I think of the other gun. The .38 he put in his mouth. One haunts. Another lays claim to memories of tracking through the forest with my brother, taking turns shooting rocks and rusted cans, just kids, when alcohol played no role in our lives.

Learning to use and respect firearms is a rite of passage on my father's side of the family, hunters raised in the backwoods of Oregon. If they didn't hunt, they didn't eat, and what little meat for sale in the nearest town's market would've been too expensive.

"You always double check the chamber when you start and when you finish. You walk with the barrel skyward or aimed at the ground. Guns," my father says, "are designed for one thing, and that's to kill. The smallest mistake can cost you or someone else their life." He pumps the rifle, throwing a shell into the chamber, places it on safety, and hands it to me. "Cradle the stock to your cheek and sight down to the bead at the end of the barrel. You want that bead square in the middle of that can on the rock. Never put your finger on the trigger until you're ready to fire."

I listen carefully, proud that he trusts me with such great responsibility.

Now I pass this rifle on to my sons, along with the same lessons in safety. Though this is a fine gun for hunting small game—rabbit, say, or squirrel—I've never used it for anything except target practice. Fishing excluded, I have trouble with the idea of killing for sport. And my father, in his later years, tells me he'd prefer to shoot a deer with a camera than a gun.

"I don't think I could pull the trigger. It just isn't in me anymore. They're so beautiful," he says.

The boys find an old wooden pallet along the side of the narrow dirt road. They drag it to the camp site, each holding one end, and set it up across the river, facing the mountainside. This way the bullets that pass through the targets, in this case tin cans they salvaged from our trash, will travel no further than the mountain, boring safely into rock and dirt. Logan is already an excellent shot, knowing the proper postures to assume for the steadiest aim, and at fifty yards or better he hits all four cans in as many tries. He clears the chamber, leaving the bolt open and pointing the barrel toward the ground as I've taught him. As my father taught me.

"Go set them up," he says to Nate.

"Why me? You knocked them down."

"Because that's how it works."

"Who says?"

"I say."

It's time for me to intervene.

"Nate," I say, "he'll have to do it next time. I'll make sure."

"Snap snap," Logan says. "Get running."

Nate gives him a dirty look and then hurries to set up the cans. Where Nate with his brown, round eyes resembles his mother, Logan takes after my Sicilian mother, the black hair and olive complexion. In some ways, when his face is turned just the right way, he reminds me of my brother, who also looked a lot like our mother. My oldest came out fair-skinned with blue-grey eyes, a throwback to both his grandfathers.

When Nate is back behind the firing line, Logan pumps a shell into the chamber, takes aim and misses. But the next shots find their mark, and now it's his brother's turn to shoot. After Logan sets the cans up, when he's behind the firing line, I give Nate the safety lesson I've given him several times before, once at a shooting range, the others at home. The gun is too big for him, so the stock has to go under his arm instead of against his shoulder, and because of this disadvantage I show him how to sit with it, balancing the barrel on his knee for a steadier aim, what is called a three-point stance. He already knows how to sight down on his target. In his first three shots, he knocks down one can. In the next five, he takes down the others.

He looks at me.

He smiles, and in that moment I see a part of me, at his age, driven by the need to prove myself to my father and brother. I remember it well. I remember wanting nothing more than to please them. To shoot as good. To catch as many fish and just as big. To keep up with them on hikes without whining even though I'm thirsty and exhausted. Complaining, if I want their respect, is not an option.

Then Nate turns his smile onto Logan, only it's suddenly a smug one.

"Snap snap," he says. "Get running."

* * *

This is the third and last afternoon that we spend on the Chetco River. Logan is taking a nap in the tent he shares with his brother. Nate is at the river's edge stacking rocks in a circle, building a prison for the brown salamanders he catches. At last count he had twenty-nine, but they keep escaping, either under or over the rocks. While he is reinforcing the walls of his salamander prison, I go to the truck for the box containing my brother's ashes. Taped to one side is an envelope, which I remove and split open. In it I find a legal document, a "Permit for Disposition of Human Remains," with the decedent listed as Donald Barry Brown, his race, dates of death and birth. Age: 27. Beneath that is the signature of the local Registrar issuing the permit, a name I can't quite make out, followed by the signature of the Funeral Director at Forest Lawn Memorial Park in neatly written script. At the bottom is our father's signature, acknowledging receipt of this document, and I wonder what it was like for him, to sign off on your son's remains. I still see him at that same kitchen table where he talked of this river, only the table is in a different house, and he and Aileen are married. Just hours before, in the early morning, two police officers came to the door with news of his son, and now he sits with his head in his hands and a fifth of Canadian Club in front of him. He's crying silently. I go to his side. I put my arm around him, and when he looks up I see the anguish and pain in the bloodshot eyes of a broken man.

"Why?" he says. "Why?"

In the coming months, grief will age him years.

Of course I did not file a permit for the disposition of my brother's remains with the Oregon Department of Health and Safety. Of course I did not file a permit for the disposition of my father's remains with the Oregon Department of Health and Safety when I scattered them here twelve years ago. This river belongs to them as much as anyone else, even more in my father's case, for to him this is the river of dreams. The river of stories. The river of his childhood.

I walk to the water's edge and remove my shoes. The rocks beneath my feet are smooth. The river pushes against the back of my legs as I move toward a deep pool of calm water that slowly empties out into the rapids ahead. Soon I am up to my waist, and the river bed has become soft with sand.

I close my eyes.

I pray, as I prayed for our father. I do not know who or what I am praying to, but I pray nonetheless. I pray with gratitude for the time Barry and I had together, however brief, and I tell him I love him, as I told my father. That I never stopped loving them. I pray for my sister, too, and that she passed quickly, mercifully. I pray that they are free of all pain and suffering. I pray for the ability to forgive. Then I open my eyes. I open the box.

Cancer took our father at seventy-six, and for Barry, depressed and alcoholic, it came by his own hand, a single shot to the head. I've waited years to scatter these ashes because I had hoped my sister would join me, that we could all make this trip together, my boys and her daughter. She loved my kids, and when she was sober she sometimes had them over for the weekend. She rented scary movies. She made bowls and bowls of buttery popcorn. Once she took them to a nearby circus and Andy won a goldfish. But she always found some excuse, some reason to postpone this trip, and now she's gone, too, another suicide. I would like to spread her ashes and Barry's together but my niece has them and |we are on uncertain terms. I know her answer without asking.

The river is cold.

The ash and bone are a dull white. I wade further into the pool and spread this ash, this bone, a handful at a time across the waters. The heavier particles float to the bottom and the lighter slowly ride the surface toward the rapids. In letting go

I feel, oddly, that I am strengthening my hold on everyone dearest to me, both the living and the dead. I am and am not alone. The Chetco remains, always running and going, joining my brother with my father, my father with my brother, and I trust that one day I will follow this river with them.

* * *

This winter the salmon will travel thousands of miles across the ocean to reach the freshwater breeding grounds of their birth. They are guided, my father told me, by the sun, the stars, and the magnetic pull of the earth. As a boy, he fished here with his father, at the mouth of the river, when the salmon came. Like the Chetco Indians hundreds of years before, my father and his father used spears to stab them, fat thirty-pounders, and snatch them out of the water. They ran so thick, he said, you could almost walk across them. Once he speared one too big and strong for him, and if not for his father grabbing his arm, it would've pulled him in.

Someday I'd like to spear salmon.

Someday, when we take this trip again, maybe my niece will allow me to spread her mother's ashes. These are my thoughts as we're packing to leave, rolling up the sleeping bags, taking down the tents. It's early in the morning and a light rain has begun to fall.

On the ride back, I will stop at The Trees of Mystery, a wonderful tourist trap off Highway 101, where my father stopped for us. I will snap a picture of my kids, as he did for his, standing together in front of the fifty-foot statue of Paul Bunyan and his thirty-five foot sidekick, Babe the Blue Ox.

Then I will pay the price of admission and show them the largest living things on earth. The Sequoia named by the

Cherokee. The Dawn and Coastal Redwood. Some are taller than the Statue of Liberty and bigger around than a tractor-trailer. They have survived floods, violent storms, and earthquakes, and when one dies and falls, the limbs and roots feed from the trunk and become many trees. As we wander this forest, I will search for the awe in their eyes as I'm sure our father searched for the awe in ours.

Later, back in the car, I will tell my sons stories about the grandfather they never met, the uncle they never knew, the aunt who left them too few memories. I will talk about their mother as well, especially their mother, and how she loved them, how that love now resides in the heart. I need for them to remember. I need for all of us to remember, even if it's only a story, and I hope to return to the Chetco with all three of my boys. I hope, someday, for us all to stand on the banks of this river, spears in hand, poised to throw, as the rush of salmon make their final way home.

DIRTY MOVES

At 4:30 on a Sunday morning, I roust my boys out of bed and tell them to use the bathroom. When they're done, each takes his turn stepping onto the scale beside the tub. They're groggy, of course. They're slow to react but they don't protest. My older son understands the importance of a single ounce and the younger is quickly learning. The slightest difference in weight can mean having to compete in the next division, potentially giving away nearly five precious pounds to your opponent. That might not sound like much, but it is, when you're already little more than muscle and bone. This is about real wrestling, not the theater you see on TV with heavily-muscled men flinging each other around a ring.

Stripped to his boxers, Logan tops the scale at 111 pounds. He's an ounce and one pound over for the division in which he prefers to wrestle, where he's strongest, between 105 and 109.

"Fuck," he says.

"Don't cuss," I say.

He steps off the scale.

"I knew I shouldn't have eaten that banana last night."

"You might still make it."

"How?"

"By the time we get there," I say, "you'll probably have to use the bathroom again. That's another three, maybe four ounces. And you can always run around the gym a couple times."

At eleven, Logan has been wrestling competitively for five years, and he does not like to come in disadvantaged in the least. Little Nate, on the other hand, is only five and weighs in at thirty-four and one-half pounds, close to the limit for his class. I pat him on the head as he steps off the scale.

"Good going," I say.

"What?"

"You're on weight."

"Oh," he says. "Is that good?"

This is his first year in competition, and he's excited, wanting to follow in his brother's footsteps and win his own shelf full of medals and trophies. I'm confident that he will. The youngest in the brood is often the toughest, having on a daily basis to fight off the tortures and teasing of his older brothers.

By five that morning we're in the car, starting out for El Monte High School in East Los Angeles, and every time I'm headed in this direction, toward L.A., it triggers a certain anxiety, both a longing and fear. I always think of my brother. I always think of my sister and I'm reminded, vividly, that they are no longer among the living. But today is not about them. Today is not about me and the loss of my brother and sister, and I push back against the memories. I return them, to the best of my abilities, to the darker, less accessible recesses of the mind.

It's a good seventy-mile drive, and we need to be there between six and seven for weigh-ins. Miss those and you don't wrestle. Nate is snuggled up in the back with a blanket and a pillow. Logan sits shotgun but with the seat reclined, huddled under his Levi jacket, so that he can sleep too. I sip coffee from my wife's Starbucks travel mug and try to keep my eyes open. It's not light yet, the road is empty, and as we weave our way down the mountain the shadows of the pines give way to the glow of the street lights of San Bernardino. The windows of the cheap apartments and run-down houses are still dark. Mostly it's only truckers out at this hour on a Sunday morning, and we make good time. Shortly after sunrise, we pull off the freeway, drive a few more miles, and then turn into the parking lot of the high school. Already it's beginning to fill up.

The registration tables are situated outside the main entrance to the gym. I get in line behind the other fathers and mothers and wait my turn with Nate. Logan, meanwhile, takes this opportunity to run around the gym, hoping to shed those last ounces. A few minutes later I step up to the table and show the woman in charge my kids' USA Wrestling cards.

"What team are they on?"

"We're independent."

"Excuse me?"

"We don't have a team," I say. "It's just me and my two sons."

"I'm sorry, sir," she says. "They have to be on a registered USA team or they can't wrestle."

We used to have a team but it disbanded a couple of years back when the coach's three boys graduated from USA Junior Wrestling to high school wrestling. Now, from time to time, especially when the people working the registration tables are new to their job, I have problems. But I'm prepared. I know the USA Junior Wrestling by-laws by heart, down to the page and section article number which states that independents are allowed to compete so long as they're accompanied by a registered Copper Coach with a current Copper Coach card. And that person would be me. I'm about to rattle all this off to the woman when the man working the table beside her, a man who's registered us several times in the past, speaks up.

"No, we take independents. We don't get many but we take them. I know this guy," he says. "You're from the mountains, right?"

"Lake Arrowhead."

He whistles.

"Long drive," he says.

Once I've signed them in and paid the entry fees, I searchout Logan, catching him as he rounds the corner of the gym at an even jog. He's worked up a sweat, though he's not breathing heavily, a good sign for an athlete in shape.

"Did you use the bathroom?" I ask.

"Yeah, but I barely had to go."

I look at my watch.

"Better quit running," I say. "There's only twenty minutes left for weigh-ins."

"I don't think I'll make it."

"So you wrestle up a division. It's no big deal," I say.

"You're tough."

"Yeah," he says. "Except that kid from Norwalk goes one-tens."

He's referring to the boy who beat him for first place at an earlier tournament. It was a close match, Logan leading by two points going into the last round when he took a chance, made an error, and the other kid capitalized on it.

I try to be upbeat. I try to turn his self-doubt around on him.

"That's good," I tell him.

"Why?"

"Because you need the competition. You learn more from your losses, not your wins. Besides," I say, "you'll get him this time."

Gang graffiti mars the walls outside of the boys locker room, and the lockers themselves are mostly busted and broken. This is where weigh-ins take place, and it's packed inside with kids from the competing teams. The Outkasts. The Terminators. The Fontana Boyz and the Scorpions. All have team warm-up suits while my sons are simply dressed in jeans and T-shirts. Obviously we stand out, and not solely for lack of uniforms. We are one of the few white families in an overwhelmingly Mexican-American community. I don't know if it's my imagination or not, if I invite it somehow, or if it's just part and parcel to the nature of wrestling, but we occasionally get that dirty, lingering look that suggests we're not welcome here.

In the last ten years or so, wrestling has also become more popular with girls, which is terrific, but because of their presence in the locker room, and they're only a few here this morning, it's mandatory that the boys weigh-in wearing their singlets. For Logan, that means forsaking another couple of ounces, and sure enough, when he strips down to his singlet and steps on the scale, he's over the mark.

The man working the scale jots down Logan's weight on a clipboard. Then he writes "110 1/2" on my son's arm with a black felt-pen. Next in line is Nate, and he's been observing his brother. He knows to wait until the man signals him to step forward, and I admire this about him, that at six he's already well mannered and mindful of his surroundings. He weighs in at thirty-four pounds, meaning he'll wrestle 30s. The divisions are separated by five pound increments.

As my boys are putting their clothes back on, I notice Logan staring at something, his eyes narrowed. I look in the same direction. The kid from Norwalk is staring back at him, just as meanly, from the other end of the locker room. I put my hand on Logan's shoulder, which seems to break the spell.

"What're you doing?"

"He's trying to psyche me out."

"Don't go there with him," I say. "Don't let him rattle you."

"I'll kick his ass."

"You're here to wrestle," I tell him, "not fight. That's exactly what he wants you to do—lose your temper and screw up."

But I can see he's not listening. I know my son well. We're very much alike in temperament, quick to anger, and when he gets like this it's impossible to reach him. For better or worse, and I suspect it's for the worse, this ugly thing will just have to run its course.

* * *

The younger children, between the ages of five and eleven, wrestle in the morning. The older ones, twelve to fifteen, compete in the afternoon. In Nate's first match he goes up against a tough little kid from the city of Fontana, birthplace of that fun-loving fraternity known as the Hells Angels. Because I am a card carrying Copper Coach who's paid all the necessary fees and dues, and attended all the mandatory seminars, I'm allowed in my son's corner on the mat. The other fathers and mothers have to stand on the sidelines, which are cordoned off with yellow caution tape, and watch the team coach instruct their sons and daughters. I hand the bout sheet to the score keepers and then take Nate aside. He's nervous, shifting his weight from one foot to the other. I kneel down so we're looking eye-to-eye.

"What's the game plan?"

"Go for points," he says. "Don't worry about the pin."

Those are my exact words.

"What else?"

"Just relax," he says, "and do my best."

"Good."

The teenage referee, likely a volunteer from the high school wrestling team here, calls Nate out to the mat. I give him a pat on the back, a gentle nudge to get him moving. The other kid is already waiting for him. He's crouched over, his knees slightly bent, hands out to his sides. It's the proper stance. Nate assumes the same position. They shake hands and then the ref blows the whistle.

It's hard to imagine brutality among six-year olds. It's hard to imagine how a coach, or a father, could in good conscience teach a child to inflict pain on another child in a fair and clean sport. But in the first round, the Fontana boy tries to bend Nate's arm, and when he can't do it, because Nate is holding strong, he strikes him in the crook of the elbow. Once. Twice. Three times. The ref is slow to respond, and when he finally does, when he blows his whistle, it's not even with a penalty. Then, in the second round, the kid grabs him from behind, locking his arms around Nate's waist. Leaning back, lifting him into the air, he slams my boy's face down into the mat.

I see him squint in pain.

I see him fight back the tears and I want it stopped. Right now. Intentionally hurting your opponent is not any way to win a match. This is not how I've taught my kids. Wrestling is about technique, speed, agility, strength, action and reaction, offense and defense, neutralizing your opponent's moves and countering if he succeeds. That slamming can merit a penalty for unnecessary roughness, which the ref again fails to note, is beside the point. I'm a second away from calling the match when I see it, this glint in Nate's eye, his face suddenly hardened with resolve. The boy is on top of him, and Nate locks the kid's arm under his own and rolls him, perfectly, onto his back for a one-point reversal and three point near-fall. The round ends a moment later, and Nate returns to his corner.

I drop to one knee, so he can hear me better.

"You're doing great. That kid's a dirty wrestler but you're smarter, you're faster. This is the last round," I say, "and you're behind by two points. I want you to go for the take-downs. Don't worry about anything else. He's leading too far with the left leg and that's what you want. That left leg. After you take him down, let him back up, okay?"

"Let him back up?

"Right."

"What for?

"Because you're going to take him down again. Only the second time," I say, "I want you to hang on, just ride him out till it's over. Escapes are only worth one point and take-downs are worth two, and you're going to win this match by one point."

And that's what he does.

When it's over, Nate walks off the mat victorious, smiling proudly. Unfortunately his next couple of bouts are even tougher, though by no means violent like the first. He loses two by narrow margins but wins his last by a pin and earns himself a fifth place ribbon out of the twelve in his division. Not bad for his first tournament. Logan wrestles later that afternoon, winning three in a row and qualifying for the final bout for first or second place in the 110 weight class. His opponent, of course, is the boy from Norwalk, who has also won three in a row, all pins.

In Logan's corner, as I'm rubbing his arms, loosening him up, I tell him pretty much what I told his brother.

"Go for the take-downs. Go for rolls and reversals. If the pin presents itself, great. But this kid is strong. Don't butt heads with him."

"I'm stronger."

"You probably are," I say, though I'm not so sure. "I want to see some good smart wrestling out there, not some wild brawl."

Unlike street fighting, there are rules here, but I'm worried that this could turn into a free-for-all. The ref hands him a strip of red Velcro, which Logan wraps around his ankle, identifying him for the score keepers. The kid from Norwalk hustles out, waving his arms, doing a kind of goose step. He's cocky. He's arrogant, and I want for Logan to knock that ego down a few notches. If nothing else, it will serve the kid well later in life.

They shake hands.

The ref blows the whistle, and Logan shoots in, not wasting a second, catching the boy off guard and taking him down for two quick points. I'm on the sidelines, excited now.

"All right," I shout. "Now turn him. Get him on his back."

In the heat of battle, and given the head gear that wrestlers wear to protect against cauliflower ears, I doubt he hears much of what I say. Of course that doesn't stop me from trying, and I continue to shout instructions from the sidelines, as does the opposing coach, a stout, pot-bellied man with a shaved head and sporting a goatee. The kid escapes and gets to his feet, but not before Logan rocks him onto his back, scoring a near-fall for another three points. The first round ends with my boy leading five to one. Logan returns to his corner breathing hard.

I hug him.

"Good work," I say. "Another take-down and that'll put you ahead seven to one. Lock him up. Ride him through the second round. Got that?"

Logan nods.

"Keep that lead going into the third," I say, "and it's over."

The rest period ends. Logan returns to the mat, and about halfway through the second round he scores yet another take down. I suck in a deep breath. I let it out slowly. There's no way, assuming he doesn't get pinned, that the other kid can catch up. Logan's done it. He's won, and I'm proud of him.

That he didn't lose his cool. That he wrestled smart.

Then something happens. Something bad.

The kid works himself free. The kid scrambles to his feet, and I don't believe that what happens next is an accident. I don't believe that his hand catching in my son's headgear is an innocent mistake, any more than I do his pulling the straps down across Logan's eyes, blinding him, and why the ref doesn't call it for what it is—a blatant foul—is beyond me. Logan takes it for granted, as any good wrestler might, that the ref will shout for time-out, and it costs him, this assumption, this belief that sport is fair. It's a troubling but necessary lesson, and I blame myself for Logan having to learn it this way, for my not having taught him earlier that in wrestling, like a lot of things, you sometimes have to assume the worst in a person.

Dazed, confused, he stands up straight, and the other kid rushes him, like a lineman taking out a quarterback. He rams him in the stomach. As his back strikes the mat, I actually hear the swell of air forced from his lungs, and inside of five seconds the referee blows the whistle. Logan's been pinned. He gets to his feet and rips off the red Velcro strip from around his ankle and throws it in the ref's face. That's when I snap, when the other coach, the guy with the goatee, starts screaming at my son.

"You apologize," he says.

"Go to hell," Logan says.

He steps toward my son, but I'm there now, in-between them.

"You discipline your kid," I say. "I'll discipline mine."

"Your boy's a sore loser."

"Your boy's a dirty cheater."

For a few seconds we just stare each other down. I know I've crossed a line I should never cross, especially in front of my children. He turns away, and it's good, because I wasn't about to.

* * *

On the ride home later that afternoon I ask my sons what they'd like for dinner. This is tradition. This is my offer after every tournament, win or lose, as a reward to us all for a day well spent together. Typically, from Logan anyway, it invites a single word—steak, say, or shrimp. He loves both. The only restriction on this offer is that it not be fast food, and it's not necessarily because I'm against it, diet-wise, because I'm not. I just like to cook for my boys. I just feel it's worth more than peeling off a few bucks to a kid in a paper hat.

Today, however, when I pop the question, I receive no answer. I look at Nate in the rearview mirror. Already a welt is forming above his left eye—the result, I imagine, of a well placed elbow or knee to the face, a blow I hadn't noticed. His arm, where the first kid struck him, is also bruised and sore. I watch him rub it. I watch him bend it up and down, slowly, like it must hurt.

"How about you?" I say. "Want anything special for dinner?"

All I get is a shrug.

For a while I let it go. For a while we drive in silence. Logan is pretty beat up, too, with bruised ribs where that kid speared him, and, from another bout, scratches on his neck and down one side of his face. I wonder if it's worth it, this wrestling, if maybe it's time we thought about hanging it up. I don't want to ask the question, because it's always been my favorite sport, because I used to wrestle. And because I liked it and was good at it, I want the same for my boys—for them to excel as wrestlers, to enjoy what I enjoyed. But if today is any indication of what's to come, I worry that they might get seriously hurt, and that concern supersedes all others. "Maybe we should try something else," I say. "Like soccer. Or baseball."

"What're you talking about?" Logan says.

"We don't have to wrestle, you know. There are other sports. Andy gave it up around your age." Andy is their older brother and they both look up to him. "It's not a big deal."

"No way," he says. "I'm nailing that fucking Mexican next time."

Half my childhood was spent in Los Angeles, the other half in East San Jose. My stepmother is Mexican. My stepbrother and stepsister are Mexican, and two of my lifelong best friends are Mexican, one so close to the family the boys call him Uncle Orlando. The other, Manuel, was my Best Man. But having attended schools made up mostly of Latinos, I also know what it's like to be hated because of the color of my skin. Pinche gavacho. White Boy. I know what it's like to be picked on, to fight, to be beaten and to beat others, and to beat them good so they would remember me. At the same time, I've experienced through family and friends the sort of acceptance and love that transcends the illness of bigotry and violence. My son, I think, ought to know better. I raise my voice.

"What'd you just say?"

He bows his head.

"Nothing," he says.

"I don't want to hear you talk like that. You understand me. No more cussing, either. I've had it." He's quiet. I shake my head. I look at him again, hard. "You're mad because he cheated. That's it. That's all. Don't get it mixed up. Mexican has nothing to do with it."

I like to believe my own words, and in this instance I do. I would like to believe that I can offer my sons a better world where there is no racism, no cheaters, no parents who teach their children to hate and hurt others. But I can offer them no such thing. At best, I can only instruct so that they might suffer less, and so that in surviving they know when to suspend the rules, for their own protection, when those rules have first been suspended against them. As we drive home that evening, both boys staring silently out the window, bruised and shaken, I make them a promise.

We will have steak tonight.

We will have shrimp, too. The works. And afterwards, when calm has prevailed, I will lead them to the middle of the living room floor and lovingly teach them the moves I eventually had to learn. Those dirty ones, the kind designed to hurt.

Some Kind of Animal

My obsession with muscle comes to an abrupt and sudden end along a narrow, two-lane mountain highway in the San Bernardino Mountains. Elevation 5,500 feet. Dead of winter. Here I am far removed from the cities and suburban sprawl of the low lands of Southern California. The night before it snowed lightly and the limbs of the pines bordering the highway are white with frost. It's a beautiful sight, how the branches shimmer in the morning sun, but the roads are treacherous, slick with black ice, the most dangerous kind because it blends into the asphalt. A shining fine veneer. You can barely see it, if you can see it at all. In years past, I've spun out on it and nearly wrecked my car, so I've learned to drive carefully. I'm making slow but safe progress when a Dodge Ram suddenly appears in my rearview mirror.

I ignore it.

Soon I look for a place to turn out and let him by, but there is none. As we continue down the highway he edges closer and closer to my bumper until his big front grill fills my back window. My heart begins to pound, and I ease up on the accelerator. That's when he flips on his high-beams and two sets of fog lamps. Together they are blinding. My face feels hot. My ears ring and then, without further warning, I snap. When he lays on his horn I pull the wheel hard to the left, so that the car spins sideways, blocking both lanes and trapping him. Now I have the son of a bitch, and I don't care how big he is. I don't care if he's a tough guy or a coward.

I jump out of my car. I want blood.

* * *

At the time of this altercation, I am bench pressing 325 pounds. I am squatting close to 400, and have, according to Paula, no visible neck. At 5'8", I weigh 195 pounds, nearly all of it muscle, no small achievement for a guy who only ten months earlier topped the scales at a mere 150.

It would be convenient, in terms of a psychological profile, to suggest that my obsession with muscle stems from an inferiority complex related to my short stature. But that would be only partially true, for it is a combination of factors that fuel my passion, among them middle age. At forty-two I feel that I'm losing my edge. I'm not as energetic. I fatigue more easily and my sexual drive isn't what it used to be. To compound matters, I have, for the better part of my life, strayed as far from the path of physical and mental health as one possibly can without entirely self-destructing. That is to say, I spent the majority of my years on this planet under the influence of various and sundry illicit substances, all of which extracted a heavy toll on my body. When I "bottom out," as they say in Alcoholics Anonymous, Narcotics Anonymous, and Cocaine Anonymous—I've earned lifetime memberships in them all—I am a pale, gaunt, middle-aged English professor with stick-like arms and a pencil-thin neck.

My goal, other than to stay sober, is to rebuild the body I'd ravaged with booze and dope. At first all I want is to feel and look healthy, maybe tone my body and get my wind back. For the average man, achieving these goals would seem more than enough. After all, most men would kill just to lose their pot bellies, let alone add a couple of inches of muscle to their arms. And under normal circumstances, for the normal person, this is where it would stop. This is where you're supposed to be happy with the improvements you've made and work now only to maintain them.

But I am not a normal person.

I have what in layman terms is called an addictive personality, and what I do, basically, is transfer my addiction to booze and dope to the seemingly healthier obsession of pumping iron.

I work out like a demon, two hours a day, five days a week. I eat well. I get eight hours of sleep every night. I subscribe to Muscle & Fitness and Flex magazine. I drink foul tasting protein shakes and spend a small fortune on body building supplements whose companies make ridiculous claims and promises when in fact their products deliver very little. After six months of intense, grueling workouts, I gain a measly seven pounds.

The solution, I think, is to work out even harder, and so I do. Longer hours. Heavier weights. After a couple of months with this approach, I actually *lose* several pounds and every day feel drained and worn out, like I have a perpetual hangover. It's called over-training, and I later learn that it has the reverse effect on muscle, causing it to weaken rather than grow.

In the beginning I admire the guys with lean hard bodies, and I want to look like them, but as time passes I find myself intrigued with the more muscular physiques of the hard-core bodybuilders. The wide shoulders and broad chest and steel-hard biceps. The thick legs. The defined, horseshoe shape of the triceps. The freaky veins popping out of the forearms and the stripped pattern of striated muscle. I like the idea of power. I like the idea of strength. This is also around the time when I notice that these bigger guys don't work out as hard as me and yet they make more gains. Where they're benching 300 or 400 pounds, I'm stuck at 200, and have been for months. No matter how hard I try, I just can't seem to break past that 200 mark, and I don't understand what I'm doing wrong. Am I over the hill at forty-two? Do I lack testosterone? Is it the curse of bad genes? I have no answers, but over the course of the next several weeks I make friends with one of these bigger guys. For reasons of privacy, I won't divulge his real name, though I will say that among the gym rats he is endearingly referred to as Oak Junior, named after his idol, Arnold Schwarzenegger, the original Oak and Governor of this Golden State.

One morning he asks me to spot him on the bench press. He has eight plates on the bar for a total weight of 405 pounds. This is a warm up.

"I'm going for eight reps," he says.

Without breaking a sweat, he knocks them off. I shake my head in amazement. Then I ask him, point blank, how he does it. How he got so strong, so big. Oak Junior laughs. He has two words for me.

"The Juice."

"What?"

"D-Bol, man," he says. "The Big E. Deca. Winnie-V. Tes-C." He looks me up and down and smiles. "No offense, but a few years ago I was a skinny little geek like you."

I ignore the insult.

What peaks my interest are those strange sounding names. I have no idea what they mean, but I'll find out soon enough, when Oak Junior and I make a run to Mexico. The drive takes about two hours from my home in the mountains, down through the flatlands and across the desert to the cool breeze blowing off the coast of San Diego. From here it's only a couple of miles to the border and another to the main drag, Revolucion Boulevard, in Tijuana. The streets are lined with pharmacies, and tourist shops offering leather vests, jackets, cheap jewelry, and switchblades. I follow Oak Junior through the crowded sidewalks, down another block, off the beaten path and into an animal supply and feed store.

"What're we doing here?" I ask.

But Oak Junior ignores me. In a place like this, I'd expect to find Mexican farmers and ranchers, and there are two or three, but the others are all Americans—two teenagers, one young woman with abnormally large biceps, and three clean-cut burly guys. Cops, I think. In Southern California, it's rumored that many are on the juice.

The store smells of alfalfa and barnyard manure. Behind us, stacked on top of each other, are cages with parakeets, puppies, rabbits, and ducks, and secured in a glass case nearby are the accoutrements of rooster fighting—the shiny chromed spikes, razors, and gaffs that attach to the leg of the gamecock. And behind the counter, directly ahead of us, are shelves and shelves of little bottles and boxes. Oak Junior points to one and the clerk passes it to him.

"This is good shit," he says to me.

But it has the picture of an animal on the label. I look more closely.

"That's a dog," I say.

He shrugs and turns the box over. On that side it has the picture of a bull.

"Dog, bull, what's the difference? It all works the same."

The substance is straight, unadulterated testosterone. We buy that and more, and later on the ride back home I learn, for instance, that the Big E stands for Equipoise, a steroid given to race horses, as is Winnie-V, chemically known as Stanazol. And D-Bol, a long time staple of the athletic community, is equally popular in the cattle industry. All of these drugs are injected with a syringe. All of these drugs are "stacked," administered together in various dosages and combinations, making for a potent steroid cocktail.

In the days to come I learn when and where to best stick myself with the needle: it's typically done on a weekly basis, shooting directly into a muscle, the least painful area being the buttocks. Most importantly, Oak Junior schools me on the host of other drugs you need to counter the potential side-effects of steroid use. For testicle shrinkage, you take the fertility drug, Human Chorioic Gonadrotropin, or simply HCG, which is manufactured from the urine of pregnant women. To combat gynecomastia, otherwise known in body building circles as "bitch tits," you need Clomid, another fertility drug used to induce ovulation in women. For water retention, a common side effect of testosterone usage, you take the powerful diuretic Lasix, normally prescribed for edema and high blood pressure.

In six months, armed with this knowledge, I'm benching 300 and have gained twenty-five pounds. My medium-sized shirts no longer fit. I can't get into my regular 501's anymore and have to buy relaxed-fit. As for my boxers, they go into the rag pile, too, because I can't get them around my thighs without cutting off the circulation.

Paula feels compelled to enlighten me one evening. We are stretched out in bed, having just made love for the second time in the last hour or so. For sex drive, certain steroids, especially injectable testosterone, are superior to the fleeting effects of Viagra and its rivals. "Look at your legs," she says.

"What about them?"

She makes a face.

"It's like they're growing tumors."

She is referring to my vastus lateralis, that is to say the outer thigh muscle, for which I am quite proud of having developed.

"And your shoulders, too. You better stop taking that stuff. Seriously," she says, "you're starting to look like some kind of animal."

I draw my hand along her arm. I let it slide down between her legs and she pushes me away.

"Enough is enough," she says. "Leave me alone. It isn't fun anymore."

Then she rolls out of bed and begins to dress. I reluctantly do the same, and as I'm slipping into my relaxed-fit Levis I glance at myself in the dresser mirror. The comment she'd made seems far-fetched. I take pride in those tumors in my legs. I take pride in the width and girth of my shoulders and how each muscle—the anterior, medial, and posterior deltoid—are nicely defined. I admire the line of my traps, how they compliment my lats and form a clear triangle of muscle through the middle of my back. In the mirror, to my eyes, I see something completely different than my fiancé: to her I'm overblown and muscle bound, to me I look cut and solid, anything but overbuilt.

So for the next few months I continue my quest for more muscle, for that rock solid physique, and to this end I increase the length and intensity of my workouts. I increase the dosages of steroids. And because protein is the building block for muscle, I increase my diet, too. I eat like a pig. Each morning, I consume a dozen egg whites and wash them down with a quart of milk. At lunch, I devour two or three chicken or tuna sandwiches and put away another quart of milk. For dinner, moreoften than not, I eat blood rare steaks.

I grow.

Like a bull, I think. Big. Strong.

Now I wear an extra large T-shirt. The once loose, relaxed-fit Levis are no longer loose or relaxed. Instead, they are skin-tight, and the inside of my thighs rub together when I walk. Evidently, at least to others, I've undergone a radical physical mutation, but less noticeably, at least to myself, I experience another, more insidious sort of metamorphosis.

With the increased energy level from the steroids, almost like a speed high, I sleep on average about four to five hours a night. Of course that sort of schedule eventually takes a toll on my moods which, given my psychological condition, are not altogether stable in the first place, and I often find myself irritated by things that never used to bother me before.

I'm short with friends.

I'm short with colleagues, and in the classroom, when I'm teaching, I become increasingly less patient with my students. My temper is not, as they say, at a slow boil: one second I can be perfectly calm, and then, in the next, I might lose it. Once, while I'm reading the newspaper, I come across an article that upsets me, something to do with politics, and I throw the paper on the floor and begin stomping on it, jumping up and down when Paula happens into the room.

"What're you doing?"

"Nothing," I say, sheepishly.

"Look at you," she says. "Your face is all red. You're sweating."

"I'm just a little upset."

"Jim," she says, "it's not normal to get that crazy over the newspaper. Don't you see what those steroids are doing to you?"

"I'm fine."

"All you've done is switched one drug for another."

"Steroids aren't drugs," I say. "I know my drugs and they're not drugs."

"Go ahead, keep lying to yourself. Keep letting those steroids make you rage like a lunatic."

Of course, like any good alcoholic or addict, I'm well practiced in the art of denial, and I can't for the life of me see how steroids do anything except build muscle. I do concede, however, that they can on occasion increase aggressiveness. But now that it's been pointed out to me, and if I make a concerted effort to remain conscious of it, I feel I'm perfectly capable of keeping my temper in check. So as far as I'm concerned, Paula is blowing this entire incident totally out of proportion.

"Relax," I tell her. "I have everything under control."

* * *

Under normal circumstances, I rarely act on my hostile impulses. I may get mad, even furious, and on occasion justifiably so, but my better judgment in such matters typically prevails. Unfortunately the incident along that narrow, two-lane mountain road is not one of these times. Imbued with a sense of invincibility, my anger fueled by steroids, I approach the Dodge Ram and yank open the door.

Techno music blasts from inside. He's just a kid, nineteen at most. He throws his hands up in front of his face.

"Hey, take it easy," he says. "I didn't mean nothing, man."

I grab him around the throat with one hand. He has on a baseball cap turned backwards and it falls off. I look him hard in the eyes.

"Stay off my ass," I say.

The kid doesn't move, not even to try and break away. It might've ended there, and I wish it had. But when I let him go, as I start back to my car, he opens his fool mouth.

"Fuck you," he says.

I turn around.

"What'd you say?"

"You heard me, asshole."

In a matter of seconds, he's gone from being fearful to defiant, and it's a big mistake, one that costs us both. On this lonely road dusted with snow, in a place of quiet and peace, I walk back to his truck. I reach for his neck again, only this time he pulls away and takes a swing at me. The blow glances off my arm and I grab him by the collar and yank him out of the truck. His shirt rips and he falls to the ground, and as he's getting to his feet I hit him good on the side of the head, square in the temple, then again in the nose. I feel the cartilage give under my fist and then there is blood. Lots of it. All down the front of his bright white T-shirt.

The fight could've gone on. I could've hurt him worse, and I wanted to, if not for this voice in my head telling me *no, stop, enough.* The last thing I remember about that kid are his eyes, bulging with terror. After that, it gets sketchy. I don't remember, for instance, walking back to my car. I don't remember driving off. It's called a "red-out," like the alcoholic "black-out," where there's a lapse in memory. But there's no forgetting what happened about five minutes later: just a few miles up the road the Highway Patrol pulls me over, and the next thing I know my hands are flat on the roof of his cruiser. He's patting me down.

"But it was self-defense," I lie.

As I try to talk my way out of this mess, I hear my fiancé's voice in the back of my mind. I hear her, finally, loud and clear. I am some kind of animal, rabid and enraged. Ahead the road glistens, the sun melting away the dangerous, shining veneer of black ice.

AMERICAN MARIACHI

At the door we're told to empty our pockets. Keys. Change. Anything that might set off the metal detector is placed in a plastic basket and inspected by the guard. This is the Riverside Auditorium, and my buddy Orlando and I have come together tonight for two very different fights. The main event is beamed in live by way of satellite from Caesar's Palace in Las Vegas. Julio Cesar Chavez of Mexico, the holder of six world titles, takes on Oscar De La Hoya, otherwise known as the Golden Boy from East Los Angeles. The other fight is a personal one between Orlando and his partner David. Orlando has been there for me in the toughest of times, when I've flipped or worse, and as his best friend it falls on me to soften the blow of his recent break-up with David.

"The Golden Boy goes down inside five," I say.

Orlando laughs.

"Dream on."

"Twenty bucks says I'm right."

"I hate to take your money," he says, "but if you insist."

We step up in line. The guard at the door is just a kid, eighteen or so, wearing nothing more official than a T-shirt that reads "Security" across the chest. He looks through the plastic basket Orlando passes him and plucks out a silver penknife.

"You can't go in with this."

"It's a just a penknife."

"A knife is a knife," the kid says. "No knives allowed."

The blade can't be more than a couple of inches, and it really isn't good for much other than splitting envelopes or paring fingernails. That Orlando does not in any way, shape, or form fit the profile of a man prone to stab another, even in self-defense, apparently makes no difference to this kid. A Yale graduate dressed in a Ralph Lauren polo shirt, khaki pants and loafers, Orlando resembles an average yuppie.

"Make up your mind," the guard says, "or get out of line. You're holding everybody up."

There's a cardboard box at the kid's feet, and in it are a dozen or so other knives, mostly small ones, some looking expensive. Orlando stares down at them and shakes his head. I can tell he's having second thoughts, and I can understand, because this knife once belonged to his father, who has since passed on. Parting with it is not a good idea.

"We could walk back to the car," I say, "drop it off and get in line again."

Orlando glances behind him. The column of people stretches down a long set of stairs to the sidewalk and all the way around the block. He turns and looks at the kid again.

"I get it back, right? You'll be here when the fight's over?"

"Yeah, sure," he says. "That's my job."

His tone of voice does little to inspire our confidence, but Orlando nonetheless relinquishes the knife, and we step through the metal detector. There another guard frisks us, for what I'm not sure, alcohol or drugs maybe, or some other sort of weapon. This is after all Riverside, California, the good neighbor of San Bernardino with the seventeenth highest violent crime rate in the nation. Both are desert communities residing outside the Los Angeles County line, more suburban sprawl than actual city, and each has its own vibrant, thriving nightlife of prostitutes, addicts, and homeless.

The auditorium was built in an earlier, more prosperous era that placed greater value on intricate designs, cornices and sweeping archways, pillars and stained glass. Inside, it holds two-thousand, and with fold-out chairs set up in the aisles they can squeeze in another couple of hundred or so. It's a sold-out crowd, and already the place is filling up, but we've arrived early enough to secure decent seats about a dozen rows back from the big screen. The audience is nearly all men, many heavily tattooed and sporting shaved heads, while others for the most part wear cowboy hats and cowboy boots, blue jeans and silver belt buckles. The heavy smells of various colognes and aftershave fill the air. Combined, they're enough to turn my stomach.

We settle into our seats. For a while neither of us speak. I'm busy taking in the surroundings, but Orlando, he's simply depressed.

"Hey," I say, "cheer up."

"What for?"

"Because he's not worth it."

"We were together six years. It's not like I can just forget

him overnight."

They may have been seeing each other for six years but they never took that next step of living together, which always struck me as odd, given that they loved each other. I know Orlando loved him. Still, they called each other every day, and two or three times a month, Orlando, who lives in Riverside, drove the eighty miles into Hollywood to visit him, have dinner and hit a movie, stay the night or two. Then just last week he drops by unexpectedly and finds a realtor's "For Sale" sign on the front lawn. This man he loves is getting ready to move back to New York and doesn't even bother to tell him. And it angers me. By attempting to avoid a painful confrontation, David is inadvertently choosing to inflict greater injury on my friend.

"Fuck him," I say. "It's his loss."

Orlando's employs a typical diversion tactic.

"Last chance," he says.

"For what?"

"To change your mind about the fight. I really don't want to set you back."

The auditorium lights dim. Cheers go up. People shout. People clap and yell and whistle. Boxing fans are generally a rowdy group, and the rowdiness grows in direct proportion to the caliber of the fight and the fighters. The stakes are high for

Chavez, El Grande Campeon Mexicano, considered the greatest boxer in the history of his country, putting his world welterweight title on the line against Oscar De La Hoya, the rising young star and Olympic gold medalist, one of the best of his generation, and at twenty-three already at the top of his game.

In the pre-fight images flashed onto the screen, De La Hoya assumes the classic stance, one fist to his chin, the other cocked at his side. The American flag waves in the background, rippling as it would in a strong wind, and I'm suddenly caught off guard. Two thousand voices boo and curse, drowning out the opening chords of our National Anthem, and moments later, when Chavez appears with the Mexican flag, the same crowd explodes into cheers.

I lean toward Orlando.

"The bet's off," I say.

"What?"

"I've been reborn. As of this moment I'm officially a De La Hoya fan."

Orlando gives me his trademark chuckle, the kind that suggests he understands something I don't.

"C'mon," he says, "what do you expect? They're Mexicans. Mexican-Mexicans from Mexico. It's not like they feel wanted here. Besides, who's going to do your dirty work? Mow your lawn? Bus your dishes? Give them a break. They just want a little piece of the American Pie."

He's right, I think, though I'm not about to admit it. As friends, it's best to keep the banter alive, especially on a night when Orlando is hurting. After all, we're here to enjoy ourselves, if only for so long as it takes two talented, highly skilled men to beat the living hell out of each other. The odds favor Chavez.

In over ninety bouts he's only lost once, but at thirty-five he is also at the ebb of his prime. De La Hoya, on the other hand, has just come into his own, so far undefeated with twenty-one wins, most of those knockouts. In one corner stands Chavez, representing the school of hard knocks with a nose made flat from being broken so many times, and eyes, like a pit-bull's, set wide across the skull. In the other corner stands De La Hoya, symbolizing a comparatively easier, softer life with the handsome, unmarked face of youth and privilege. For the overwhelming majority here, the measure of a man's character will be judged by his scars and bruises. They want blood tonight. They want broken bones. They want to see that pretty boy's face all messed up.

Chavez is the man to do it, and when he steps into the ring wearing a headband with the green, white, and red stripes of the Mexican flag, the audience breaks into cheers again. De La Hoya makes his grand entrance to boos and jeers.

For the first few seconds, they circle the ring, each feeling the other out, their eyes locked. The Golden Boy is keenly aware of Chavez's power, particularly his left hook, probably the most devastating punch in his arsenal, one that's dropped many men, and initially De La Hoya keeps a safe distance between them. It even seems as if he might be a little scared, but that isn't the case, not at all, and while still in the early seconds of the fight, as the audience chants for its countryman, the Golden Boy lands a tremendous blow in the form of a straight jab. It splits Chavez's forehead, opening a deep cut just above the left eyebrow, and I can feel it, actually feel it, all the hope and excitement draining from the crowd. The entire auditorium falls silent. It's as if everyone is in a state of shock, unable to process what they've just witnessed. That it could possibly end this way. So soon, so suddenly, with a single punch.

This is not how a legend should go out, a bloody mess, but it doesn't get any better. De La Hoya, with his longer reach, continues to jab and move, and over the course of the next few rounds, he has Chavez bleeding from the nose and mouth. Finally, in the fourth, nearing the bell, the referee steps between them and wisely calls the fight. Slowly at first, and then more loudly, a rumbling passes through the crowd. Again I feel it, the energy around me, only this time, instead of shock and despair, it's all about anger. Someone behind us throws an empty pint bottle at the screen. Another in the front rows jumps up on his seat and starts screaming in Spanish. Hundreds of others soon join him, shouting and waving their fists in the air.

"Let's get out of here," Orlando says, and we do, pushing through the crowd, working our way toward the lobby doors. The closer we get the more people press up against us. We're barely moving, and it's hard to breathe, squeezed in by all the bodies, their heat and odors, cologne and aftershave. For us to stay together through this mess is a real struggle, but eventually we make it past the front doors and into the cool night air. Unfortunately the guard, the one who confiscated Orlando's knife, is nowhere to be found.

For five, maybe ten minutes we stand to the side, watching people push and shove their way out the doors, and when the procession begins to dwindle, we walk around the building. We're hoping to find another box office, maybe, or a security booth, something or someone who can help us out, but we come up empty handed. Even the side exits are chained, and you can hear them, the people still inside, shouting and pushing against the doors. "Hell with it," Orlando says. "I'll never see that knife again." On our way to the parking lot we hear sirens, at first faint but quickly growing louder, and sure enough, as we're pulling out in Orlando's car, heading up the street, the police cruisers begin pulling in.

On the 91, traveling in the fast lane, I look over at Orlando. He's staring straight ahead. His lips are pursed, and I sense that his anger has given way again to depression.

I tell him he's better off without this guy.

I tell him it'll take some time, yes, but he'll pull through. He managed just fine before on his own and he'll manage just fine again.

"You're a wonderful man," I say, "and someday somebody is going to come along and realize just how much you have to offer."

At Orlando's house, I retrieve my car parked in the driveway. We hug before I slip behind the wheel. "Call me, okay," I say. "I don't care what time it is, just call." But I know he won't. He tends to isolate when he's troubled, and I worry these next few months will be his toughest.

In the paper the next morning, I read that a riot broke out after we left the auditorium and that a couple of men were stabbed. I have no idea how anyone snuck in a knife, but when we watch De La Hoya fight again, around this same time the following year, it's in the comfort of Orlando's living room on pay-per-view TV. This fight is against a black guy, and we watch him head down the aisle toward the ring, the crowd booing and jeering, while James Brown's "Living in America" blasts in the background. De La Hoya comes next. The fans cheer and whistle as he climbs into the ring wearing a sombrero and a silk robe with the green, white, and red stripes of the Mexican flag. He's accompanied by a troop of mariachis blowing on big brass trumpets and strumming acoustical guitars. Orlando smiles at me, and I return it.

"Who do you want?" I say.

"The Chicano, of course."

"*Because* he's Chicano?"

"Yeah, *because* he's Chicano. Somewhere in-between, like me, not totally Mexican-Mexican and not totally American, either."

"You're as American-American as they come," I say, "and so am I." And because I'm less forgiving of De La Hoya's opportunism, I defect for the occasion from Orlando's camp of ethnic loyalties. "I'm going with the black dude," I say. Orlando just shrugs, and I wonder, if his skin was white and mine was brown, if I'd define myself as he does now.

At this point in time, he has made something of a recovery from David, but now and then I still ask about him. A few months earlier, on Orlando's 50th birthday, David sent a card and instead of "love" at the end, before signing his name, he wrote "fondly." We laughed about it, but I could see it in his eyes, that it still hurt. That he hadn't quit caring.

"Hear any more from David?"

"David who?" he says, smiling. Then he adds, "Yeah, he called from New York a couple weeks ago, but I didn't answer it. It's over, man. It was over a year before he left and I just couldn't see it."

I look back at the TV. De La Hoya sheds his robe. Seconds later the bell sounds, and they come out of their corners. They circle each other in the middle of the ring, and we watch. We watch and we joke and we talk, if only for so long as it takes two talented, highly skilled men to beat the living hell out of each other. Orlando and I, both the sons of carpenters, we are like brothers, and though we may disagree, for me there is no clash of cultures in this age-old fight tonight, no great divide. Nothing, really, so genuine as the cold hard cash that flows from the masquerade.

OUR JAPAN

It's Yukio's day to appear before the University Grade Grievance Committee. Just a few units shy of graduating, and planning to walk in June, he's failed the third and last class in a series of American Literature courses required of all English majors. The odds of a student prevailing in a grade dispute are slim at best, and most of them know better than to challenge their professors. But Yukio's in a fix. Under ordinary circumstances, he could simply retake the failed class, but this particular one is only offered once a year and that's where he runs into trouble. With his visa about to expire, and having already requested and received an earlier extension from the INS, we represent Yukio's last hope of graduating before he's expelled from the country.

For Yukio, it's a formal affair, and he brings to the meeting a certain air of deference for the committee. But he is poor and the sleeves of his dress coat fall noticeably short of his wrists. His slacks pinch at the knees and the cuffs are slightly frayed and worn. It's an old suit, maybe one picked from the racks of a thrift store, but the bright red tie is new, and it's carefully knotted. His English is at times broken. It would be a disservice to Yukio if I were to try and replicate it here.

"I can't go back to Japan," he tells us, "without my degree."

We're gathered in a cluster at the conference table with Yukio seated alone at the opposite end. There are six of us on the committee, all tenured professors from various disciplines of the school, secure in our jobs and relaxed about it. For the occasion we wear our usual, most of us choosing Levis over slacks, Nikes over dress shoes, with our button-down shirts loose and open at the throat. I can see that Yukio doesn't appreciate our informality, but we've been through so many of these meetings. We've heard it all. Every excuse. Every rationale. In this case, Yukio is asking for one of two things: either the professor of the class he flunked allows him to retake the written final for the chance of a passing grade or we, the committee, could approve a substitute course roughly equivalent in content to the one in question. He could repeat the class next quarter. He promises to work harder.

"All I need," he tells us, "is another chance."

When he's finished pleading his case, we ask him to leave the room so we can talk freely among ourselves, and it isn't long afterward that we reach our decision: allowing Yukio to retake the final exam would be unfair to those better prepared, more responsible students who passed it. And in regard to the second alternative, we decide that in waiving the course requirements for one student, we risk setting a precedent that may later come to haunt us.

We call him back into the room.

Arms to his sides, carriage erect, Yukio assumes the formal stance of a soldier at attention.

"We empathize with your situation," the chair of the committee tells him, "but had you planned your schedule more carefully, or taken your studies a little more seriously, you wouldn't be in this predicament. The committee hopes that you'll reapply and receive an additional extension on your visa."

Yukio takes the committee's decision surprisingly well, on the surface, anyway, thanking each of us individually for the time and attention we paid his concerns, then shaking our hands before he departs, quietly shutting the door behind him. Our next pressing order of business is whether to go Thai or Mexican for lunch and we spend about as much time making up our minds as we do in determining Yukio's fate. I'm not proud of it, either, and I have since come to see matters differently, how the cruelty of our disregard that afternoon wounded an already dangerously weakened man.

It's the week before Easter and the end of the academic term, and later that evening, after I've turned in my grade rosters for the quarter, I drive to the parking lot of the Twin Peaks Sheriff's station. My wife and I are in the process of divorcing, and this is our mutually agreed upon neutral pick-up and drop-off site for the children, halfway between my old house and the cramped cottage I've been renting for the last nine months with my fiancé Paula, a former student with whom I'd had an affair and fallen in love.

As usual, my wife is late. She is late often, too often for it not to be deliberate, but I know better than to complain. Anything I say that might even remotely be construed as critical will spark a confrontation, and I just don't have the heart for it anymore, the fighting, the arguing. So I light a cigarette. I settle in for the wait, and ten or fifteen minutes later she pulls into the parking lot in her SUV.

Andy sits in the front passenger seat. He's wearing headphones, probably listening to rap. At fourteen he's full of rage and anguish and he'd rather drown it out with music than confront his pain. So he pulls away, safe, if only momentarily, from the adult world of deceit and failure. In the back Nate is strapped into one of those ridiculously bulky safety seats with enough buckles and latches and snaps to restrain a full grown psychotic. He's just turned three, and beside him is our middle son, Logan, going on eight. I'm glad to see them. I'm glad to have them every weekend of the month.

They pile out of the car.

As I'm removing Nate's safety seat, so I can put it in my backseat, my wife looks around at me. She sniffs the air.

"Is that booze I smell?"

"What?" I say.

"Are you drunk?"

She knows I'm struggling. I've been struggling for years with the bottle and other substances, and after countless failed attempts to quit, I am for the first time actually making real progress. Every evening I attend an A.A. meeting. Every week I go for group and individual alcohol and drug counseling. My compulsion to drink, I'm told, is complicated by an array of long standing mental disorders, some likely inherited. Even at the tender age of six, not long after my parents divorced, I was labeled emotionally disturbed by the school psychologist and placed in a class for Special Education students.

"I've been clean and sober for a hundred and sixty-two days," I say.

"Oh really," she says. "Too bad you couldn't do it when we were still a family. You sonofabitch. You bastard."

I feel it rising inside me, the anger, a pulsing in my ears, and I want to lash out. But I don't, and this only provokes her. She is used to fighting. I am used to fighting. We have fought for years, especially toward the end of our marriage, and by not reacting to her taunts I'm breaking a familiar pattern, an ugly cycle, one not altogether unlike that of addiction. Perversely it is her way of controlling me, pushing all the right buttons, triggering my guilt and self-loathing. These are feelings that often lead me to rationalize drinking and using.

"Do you realize what hell you put me through? What you've done to your own flesh and blood? You're sick and you'll always be sick. Sober," she says. "Maybe you can make it a month or two, but you won't last."

Her words hurt because there is truth to them. I have relapsed so many times I no longer bother to keep count. From one day to the next, I cannot say with absolute certainty that I won't drink. Staying sober requires from me constant vigilance, and I am deeply shamed for the pain my failures have caused my wife and our children. For the adulterer, like the alcoholic, there can be no lasting forgiveness, no real reparation, and to believe otherwise is to believe an even greater lie.

"Could you pass a drug test?"

I don't say anything.

She climbs into her SUV. "That's what I thought," she says, just before closing the door.

* * *

Considering the unfortunate outcome of Yukio's grade grievance, I'm surprised to find his name on the roster of my advanced fiction writing course. Easter break is over, it's the first day of spring quarter classes, and as I'm taking roll I spot him seated in the back of the room, a slight, quiet, diminutive figure of a man. A loner. He sports a scraggily goatee that he likes to tug at, twisting and untwisting the longer hairs around his index finger. On the floor, close beside him, is a briefcase, and he has a habit of occasionally tapping the side of it with his shoe.

Yukio has a few years on most of my students, I'd say he's in his late twenties, but by no means is he the oldest in class.

This is the state university and we get our share of adults, serious, determined students grateful to be here. Most of have been around the block a couple of times and have some real stories to tell.

After I've taken roll, I ask for sign-ups for the workshop in which each student presents a story to the class to be critiqued. It can be grueling for the writer, having so many readers discuss your work and not being allowed to say a word in defense or explication. To avoid argument, the rules require the author remain silent until the class has had their say.

Because it's the first day, I give them their reading assignments for our next meeting and let them go early. The room is soon empty except for Yukio. He approaches my desk.

"I know you're not one of them."

"One of what?" I say.

But he doesn't say anything.

"If you mean the committee," I say, "I voted in your favor."

It's true. But I didn't fight for him, which for all practical purposes is no better than voting against him. As I'm gathering my things to leave, Yukio places his briefcase on my desk, snaps it open and pulls out an old dog-eared copy of Lucky Town, my last novel. It's been out-of-print for years.

"Will you sign it for me?"

I take the book from him.

"Where'd you find this?"

"A thrift store," he says. "On E Street."

I haven't produced a book in nearly a decade, and rather than being proud of my last one, it is instead an ugly reminder of the many years I've wasted getting loaded. I sign it on the title page, write a short note, and pass it back. "Thank you," he says, giving me two short quick nods, an abbreviated form of the Japanese bow. On the way out, he holds the door open for me. I'm hoping he'll go his own way as we start down the hall, so I can be left to my own thoughts, but for some reason he feels a need to confide in me. Venting to strangers is typical of the troubled. I know because I've done it myself.

He tells me he's not doing so well.

He tells me his apartment was burglarized last month. He says he knows who did it because he spotted his stereo in a neighboring apartment. Just by chance, the door was open as he passed by.

"I confront him, too," Yukio says, "and he denies everything."

So he calls the cops, and when they arrive he walks them down to the thief's apartment. But all they do is talk to the guy.

"They won't even search the place," he says. "They tell me to fill out forms." Then later that same night, he pulls into a gas station near where he lives in the ghettos of San Bernardino, pays the cashier seated inside the bullet-proof booth, and starts back to his car to pump his gas. Only now there's a girl filling her car with his gas, and short of yanking the nozzle from her hands, which is not a good idea because there are several large young men sitting in her car, there is nothing he can do.

"In my Japan," he says, "people don't do so many bad things. I mean we do bad things but nothing compared to California."

At the elevators, we part ways. He presses the button and waits. I turn the corner and continue down the hall to my office where I find a campus police officer standing outside the door. She is a younger woman with red hair pulled back tight into a bun.

"Professor Brown?" she says.

"Yes."

"James Brown?"

"Yes."

She hands me a manila envelope.

"I thought it'd be better to catch you at your office instead of the classroom. I'm sorry," she says. "This is one part of my job I really don't like."

The office door across from mine is open and one of my colleagues is at her desk staring at her computer screen, pretending not to notice. I appreciate the gesture. I also appreciate how the officer serves me here rather than interrupting class and humiliating me in front of my students.

When she leaves, when I'm alone in my office, I open the envelope and find a court order filed by my wife's divorce attorney. Basically it states that because I have a history of mental illness, and because I have drug and alcohol problems, I am a potential risk to the moral character, safety, and well-being of my children. I am a potential risk to myself and others, and until the court schedules a hearing on the matter, I am barred from having any contact with my ex or our kids.

No visits.

No phone calls.

No letters. Nothing. Any attempt to circumvent the order will result in my arrest.

For the last few months, I've had the boys every weekend and I don't understand why, now when I'm sober, I'm suddenly regarded as an unfit parent. This is not about protecting the children. No, I think. This is retaliation for my getting sober. This is in reaction to my not reacting, containing my rage rather than matching it with hers, and a return to our worn-out, destructive ways. This is about punishing me for having the audacity to leave her for another woman, and worse, a younger one. This is about exploiting my inability to pass a drug test. Although I've been clean for some time, meth can be detected for up to six months in the hair follicles, and she knows it. The subject was broached in the first discussions between our attorneys.

Her taking away the children is unquestionably the most violent way of inflicting pain on me.

* * *

In sharp and vivid prose, the narrator of Yukio's story describes precisely how he intends to set fires at both ends of the hall that house the offices of the faculty of the Department of English and the Dean of the College of Arts and Letters. Soon we will smell smoke. Soon the fire alarms will sound, and when we step into the hall, he picks off everyone but me with an AK-47. He describes the assault rifle in meticulous detail, from the smooth curve of its trigger to how he loads and operates it, switching over from bursts of three to fully automatic. But the kicker is that he uses our real names, and his own, too, as our trusted narrator who envisions himself an unrequited hero.

I require my students to pass out their stories one class session in advance of their workshop date. Because we only meet twice a week, this gives them plenty of time to get the work read and prepare a written critique. This also gives Yukio's story plenty of time to circulate and find its way onto the desks of our department chair and school dean whose lives he's threatened to take. Over the weekend, I get panicked calls from them both. The chair is first.

"Tell me about this guy," she says. "You're the only one he apparently doesn't want dead."

"He's a little out there," I say.

"Jesus, I know that. But do you think he's serious?"

"I wouldn't bet on it."

"Great," she says. "Now I can relax."

"I'd say it's fifty-fifty. A lot better odds than Vegas."

"This is nothing to joke about," she says. "He's complained to me twice about losing his grade grievance and he just doesn't seem to get it. Even if I wanted, I don't have the power to reverse the committee's decision. Why is it you guys in creative writing always attract the fucking crazies?"

"It's part of being a writer," I say.

She doesn't laugh.

"Listen," she says, "I phoned the campus police this morning and apparently there's no law against threatening another's life, at least not in a story billed as fiction. But that doesn't mean we don't take every threat seriously. You know what happened at Cal State Fullerton. I think you should cancel class Tuesday. Just call in sick. Take the day off."

Ignoring the story, however, is to ignore the person, and in Yukio's case that could be the same as giving him one last good shove over the edge. I tell the chair, as I will the dean later that same afternoon, that following through with Yukio's story is considerably less jeopardous than deliberately disregarding it. To appease my other students, and in all fairness to them, I'll make attendance optional that day. I won't penalize anyone for skipping out or even refusing to turn in a written critique. But I want to hold class.

"Are you sure?" she asks.

"I think it'd be a mistake not to."

By Tuesday, the word is out that class tonight is voluntary. Only eleven out of twenty-two students show up, but I anticipated even less, so I'm neither surprised nor disappointed. The workshop process is a hard one, and though I try to foster a certain balance, stressing the importance of positive commentary in something close to equal proportion with the critical, I'm not always successful. Today, because of the troubling nature of the material, I don't know what to expect.

But I'm watching Yukio closely.

The whole class is watching Yukio closely. When I ask everyone to put their desks in a circle, he positions his near the door, and of course it arouses suspicion. He does it, we think, so he can make a quick getaway. He does it in case he has to bolt.

In his story the protagonist, a young Japanese man, comes to California wide-eyed and trusting, hoping to gain from our university the necessary tools to become a writer. Along the way, however, at every turn, he encounters hostility and prejudice. His professors are rude and unsympathetic, and instead of looking at him for what he is, a foreign exchange student learning a new language, they regard him as stupid.

Outside the university, it's even worse.

His apartment is burglarized. His gasoline is stolen at the pumps. He has also been robbed and beaten bloody by a pack of roving teenagers out for a little fun. In each instance, he reports the crime to the local police, and in each instance they do nothing but take a report. And because he makes these reports, believing it the right and necessary thing to do, if only to assist the police in apprehending these criminals before they hurt someone else, he is considered a nuisance.

A bona fide nut case.

By now, the class has formed a circle and settled into their seats. I take mine across from Yukio, just one desk away, in the event I have to lunge at him. And I will, if he reaches for a weapon, or starts after a student whose critique sets him off.

"Who'd like to start?" I say.

Everyone is quiet. I wait a few seconds, and when I get no volunteers, I call on one of my better students, one who tends to preface her opening remarks with a compliment or two. That's not the case this time.

"It's definitely disturbing," she says. "I didn't even bother reading the whole thing. Since I don't have anything good to say, I don't think I'll say anything at all."

I glance at Yukio to see how he's taking it, but his face is expressionless.

I call on the next student.

"I'll pass too," he says.

This is not going well. But it's the student's right to pass, and so I move on to yet another, an older woman around my age, in her earlier forties maybe. She's returning to college after having raised a family and wants to be a high school teacher. She's also the toughest critic in class and not exactly popular with the other students because of it. She looks directly at Yukio.

"You," she says, "need to see a shrink."

I interrupt.

"Talk about the writing," I say. "Not the person."

"In this case I don't see the difference. He uses real names, and I like these professors he's talking about killing. So he's had a hard time," she says. "So fucking what? We all get kicked around in life. Just because he gets ignored and beat up doesn't give him the right to grab a gun and start shooting everybody."

Again I glance at Yukio.

Again he maintains a poker face. Clearly he's anticipated these sorts of comments and already steeled himself against them. If I detect any reaction, it's the slightest hint of a smile. But there's no smugness in it, none that I sense.

Once the older woman takes the lead, the other students voice their opinions, fast and hard and all along the same tough line. If not to defend Yukio, because I think like the class, that the story is indefensible, but as the teacher, and in the name of fairness, it nevertheless falls on me to assume the role of devil's advocate.

Any of us, I tell them, even the most sound of mind might one day find ourselves teetering on the edge. Real or invented, by no means is this character alone or unique. We all have our breaking point. We all have our limits. Who's to say how much pain and disappointment you can reasonably suffer before you snap. And why does it end on an uncertain note, when Yukio turns the gun on himself, before he pulls the trigger, if he pulls the trigger, suspended in that moment between life and death? The story is about violence, instability, anger, and anguish. It is one, I say to the class, that at some unfortunate point we may all come to know better.

"Yukio."

"Yes."

"It's your turn to talk," I say. "Do you want to add something?"

He shakes his head.

"No," he says. "No, thank you."

* * *

Years earlier, at the state university in Fullerton, California, located about sixty miles from where I teach at CSU San Bernardino, custodian Edward Charles Allaway committed the deadliest massacre in Orange County history. After phoning his estranged wife and telling her that this was his "last day to live," Allaway drove to the Fullerton campus and shot and killed seven people, including two professors. Judge Robert P. Kneeland removed all criminal penalties in Allaway's trial, finding him "not guilty by reason of insanity."

Not long after this incident, at nearby Fullerton Junior College, a male Japanese student, apparently emotionally distraught over his failing grades and his parents' high expectations for him, fatally shot his apartment manager. Afterwards, he sought refuge in a classroom with massive windows overlooking the campus where in full public view he put the gun to his head and pulled the trigger. In yet another instance, Peter Odighizuma, a forty-three year old Nigerian foreign exchange student on the verge of flunking out of law school, executed a professor and the university's dean at point-blank range. Like Edward Charles Allaway, Odighizuma was later declared mentally unfit to stand trial and found "not guilty by reason of insanity."

The list goes on, and I suppose it may never end. I also suspect that it is with knowledge of these murders that our Dean of the College of Arts and Letters has a change of heart. Two days after we workshop Yukio's story, she asks me to intervene on his behalf.

"He's a walking time bomb," she tells me, over the phone. "I want him on the next plane back to Japan as soon as possible, and if that means bending the rules, bend them."

The arrangement is this: In lieu of having to retake the class he flunked, Yukio will report directly to me in English

522: Independent Study. He'll sign a contract stipulating that he must complete several assignments the approximate equivalent of those he failed in American Lit. And it's tacitly understood between the dean, the chair, and myself that I'll pass him regardless of the quality of his work. In the spring quarter we meet twice a week for an hour in my office, and I go over his writing carefully, sentence by sentence, pointing out unsupported claims, correcting grammar, and encouraging him where and when it's due.

All during this same period of time, I have yet to see my children. The court date has been postponed again and again and it's been pulling me down, the waiting; it's been growing, the anger inside me, the sadness and frustration. Sometimes late at night, on my way home from the university, I take a detour and park on the street in front of my old house. The windows are usually dark except for a light in the kitchen, and I wonder if my wife is still awake or if the light has been left on for safety's sake. I imagine my boys sound asleep in bed. I imagine kissing them each good night, as I often did, and cuddling the youngest to my chest before placing him in the crib. Leaving my children is intensely, horribly difficult, and for many nights, as my fiancé sleeps quietly beside me, I lay awake wondering how I can justify the pain I've caused my family in the pursuit of alleviating my own.

* * *

By the end of the quarter, Yukio has earned a B, I file a Change of Grade form that the dean and chair have to sign, which they do willingly and quickly, and in June he's awarded the Bachelor of Arts in English with a concentration in Creative Writing. Now it's the day after graduation ceremonies, and as I'm gathering my things to leave for the summer, Yukio shows up at my office. Nothing has been resolved in my personal life, and I'm troubled. I'm emotionally exhausted and he can sense it.

"Are you okay, Professor Brown?"

"I'm fine," I say.

"You don't look fine," he says.

I do a quick check around the office to make sure I've locked the window, turned off the computer and printer. I close my briefcase. I shut off the light.

"I was just on my way out," I say. "You want to walk and talk."

I lock the door behind me and we head down the hall, down the stairs and out of the building. It's a smoggy day. It's a hot day in the triple digits, and if the skies were clear you'd see the San Bernardino Mountains rising from the foothills at the base of the campus. Now, with the haze so thick, you wouldn't even know the mountains were there. In my ears I suddenly feel the rapid beat of my heart, and then it's as if a flood gate has opened and I'm talking, telling him about my situation. The divorce. My wife. The loss of my boys and how powerless I feel. Frustration builds and turns to depression. Depression becomes despair, and when what little hope might remain finally dies, a dangerous fire ignites. I don't know if I'm making any sense. Everything seems told out of sequence, and I try to back up, explain that my fitness as a father is in question. That it's because I drink too much. That maybe my head isn't screwed on tight. I tell him that after a series of postponements I've finally been assured by the court that there will be no further delays. Next week I'll know one way or the other if I've lost my visitation rights. There is talk of having a neutral third party present whenever I see my sons. These visits will be reduced to a matter of hours once or twice a month.

"Maybe you should write a story about it. But don't show it to anyone," he says. "Just write it and put it away and maybe you can make something good out of it later. It might help."

We reach the parking lot, and it's mostly empty, because school is out for the summer. Beside my car is an old Pontiac Firebird, its black paint faded, squatting on its axles from the weight inside. Through the back window you can see all sorts of personal belongings piled up against the glass.

Yukio hands me a set of keys.

"I leave for Japan tomorrow," he says. "Take what you want and give the rest to the Goodwill. You can sell the car. It's not worth much but it runs. The papers are in the glove compartment. I've signed them, and I have a bike too. A nice bike for one of your sons. It's locked to the railing outside the library. The key's on the ring." He pauses. "If it wasn't for you," he tells me, "I wouldn't have graduated. You'll be okay, Professor Brown. I know you'll be okay."

I really don't want his car.

I really don't want all the stuff inside of it, either. But it wouldn't be right to say so.

The pulsing in my ears has passed as suddenly as it came over me. We shake hands. We wish each other well, and I'll never know if what he said to me about writing a story signaled a greater understanding of his own. But I would like to believe so. I would like to believe as I did then, and as I do now, that he never would've followed through on his threats. Of course I could be wrong. I could be very wrong. Pushed to the brink, denied both voice and dignity, he could've well imploded. To a degree I would understand it, and to a lesser extent even sympathize. I like to think I'm different but I am not. I could easily find myself alongside Yukio, enraged and scared and full of malice, doing more than trading stories about the potential to violence in us all.

"Be careful," I say. "Take care of yourself."

"You be careful, too, Professor Brown."

But I think we both know, as we turn and go our separate ways, that we are never truly safe, least of all from ourselves.

Instructions on the
Use of Heroin

I park behind the broken down Mercury Marquis in the driveway of my drug dealer's house. Ironically he is also my former A.A. sponsor. It's a warm summer night, and as I leave my car a couple of big mangy dogs appear from out of the darkness and begin barking. If I didn't know them I'd be scared, but I do know them because I've been here before, too many times, and they're not biters. The stairs leading to the front door are falling apart, one is missing altogether, and I step over it. The dogs are behind me all the way, sniffing at my legs.

This is not in the ghetto.

This is not the mean streets of San Bernardino, one of the most violent, drug-ridden cities in the nation. This is in the neighboring mountains well above the fray. I live safely removed from the drive-bys, the gangs, and their turf wars. In my community, you can still walk the streets at night. In my community, lakeside homes sell for millions, but even here, among the rich and middle class, there is a darker, subterranean life, and as a user of narcotics I have a special knack, a real sixth sense for rooting it out, wherever I go.

As I reach the landing at the end of the stairs, two powerful sensor lights flash on. I wince at the brightness. Then I press the button on the intercom and look up at the fake bird house mounted in the corner of the sun deck above me. Inside it is a camera, and I want my dealer to see me, so he doesn't panic and stick his 9mm in my face when I come to the door. He's done it before. There's static on the intercom, then the scratchy sound of his voice.

"Who is it?"

"It's me," I say. "Jim."

"Hang on."

On the other side of the door are three iron bars, one at the top, one in the middle, and the third near the bottom. There's also a deadbolt, a chain latch, and the regular lock. Inside I hear the clanking of the bars being removed from their steel brackets, the slam of the deadbolt, the turning of the knob, and finally the door opens a crack. The chain is still latched. He peers out at me.

"You alone?"

"Yeah," I say.

The door closes. A second later it opens again and he lets me in, along with his mangy dogs. Green garbage bags full of dirty clothes, and computer monitors, computer casings, and shells are scattered all over this downstairs area of the house. It smells, too, like urine and shit, because he sometimes forgets to let the dogs out. He's wearing a ratty tank-top, but what I notice most at this moment are the syringes hanging from his shoulders, one on each side, the needles sunk into the middle head of the deltoid muscle. On the left, it's loaded with heroin.

On the right, it's cocaine. I can tell the difference because one syringe contains a dark colored fluid while the other, the coke, is a milky white.

If he needs a bump up, he depresses the plunger on the milky white side. If he needs a bump down, something to even him out, to take the edge off the coke, it's the dark side. The idea is to find the perfect balance, but for now he's on the upside, spun on the coke.

To protect his privacy, if only in memory, because he is dead as I make record of this story many years after the fact, I'll give him another name, something common—Eddie. In addition to being a dealer he is also a friend. We met at an Alcoholics Anonymous meeting, and for nearly ten months, before we both relapsed, he'd been my sponsor, taking me through the Big Book several hours every week, page by page. He isn't looking so good lately, little more than skin and bone. We shake hands and I follow him upstairs to the living room.

Eddie gets right down to business.

"What do you want?"

"What do you have?"

"Black," he says. "Crack. Coke. Crystal. Weed. I got Diludid. I got methadone, too," he says, "Valium, Vicodin, and Oxycontin."

Diludid is like pharmaceutical-grade heroin, some junkies think it's even better, and most users already know about Valium, Vicodin, and Oxycontin. Eddie suffers from a serious back injury, and after years of unsuccessful operations, his doctors now more or less prescribe whatever he wants in the line of opioid pain killers. Combine these with his black market dope and you have a walking, talking poster boy for the travails of addiction.

"Some black," I say.

"Any weed?"

In a room upstairs, Eddie has a farm of marijuana thriving under dozens of grow lights, and he's always trying to push some off on me. But I'm scared of weed. It makes me paranoid. It makes me think, and thinking often depresses me, and depression isn't exactly what I look for in the pursuit of getting fucked up. The same goes for psychedelics. I swore them off at the age of seventeen after a bad trip.

"You know I hate that shit."

He laughs.

"Just asking."

"All I want is black."

"No coke either."

"Not tonight."

"How much you want?"

"A gram," I say.

At that, he disappears into another part of the house to retrieve the dope from its hiding spot, his gram scale, and the various other accoutrements of hardcore narcotic use. I sit down on the couch. An old episode of *Gilligan's Island* plays on the TV. The Skipper is chasing Gilligan in circles around a coconut tree, and I watch them, trying to take my mind off the waiting. Soon Eddie returns.

Clearing a spot on the coffee table, which is a mess of empty beer cans and bottles and ashtrays full of butts, he sets up his scale.

"This is good stuff," he says.

This stuff is Mexican Black, mostly commonly referred to as tar. In its uncooked form, it resembles a lump of brown dirt, but it turns black, like tar, when you heat it up.

From his front pocket Eddie takes out a knife. From his back pocket he removes a plastic baggie and a couple of packaged syringes, small ones, the kind diabetics use. Then he sits down on the couch beside me. I lean forward as he dips the tip of the knife into the baggie, scoops out a chunk of heroin about the size of a dime, and slips it onto the scale. While he weighs it, he glances up at me.

"You in the market for an AK?" he says. "I got a friend who's looking to unload an M-16, fully automatic. He has an Uzi, too, with the Israeli Army stamp on the side. A thousand bucks. And hand grenades, they go for eighty a piece or seventy by the dozen."

I have to think about it. A part of me would like to own an assault rifle or a little Uzi. The other part warns me off. I have no idea where I could even go to fire one. These aren't the kind of weapons you take to your local shooting range. The grenades, they plain scare me.

"It's tempting," I say. "But I'll pass."

I stand up and open my wallet and drop two twenties on the table. Then I go to the kitchen and come back with a glass of water and a spoon. By now Eddie has weighed out my purchase, and from it, before he wraps it up, I pinch off a small chunk. He shakes his head. "You can always put more in," he says, "but you can't take it out. I'd use about half that first and see how it hits you. This batch is stronger than the last." Of course I take his word for it. Eddie has been slamming dope off and on now for over thirty years, and until the last time he shot up, a week after he was released from prison on a possession for distribution charge, the fix that killed him, he'd never before o.d.'d. It's a ritual, from weighing the junk to parceling it out and cooking it, and this process heightens the urgency of the act, from the anticipation of the rush to its delivery, the climax of finally shooting up. The procedure is simple: You place a small lump of junk into the spoon along with a piece of cotton, if you have any handy, or just a bit torn from a cigarette filter. Then you add a little water to it. Next you heat it up with a lighter, holding the flame under the spoon. When it begins to bubble and liquefy, you insert the needle into the cotton or the bit of cigarette filter and draw it out into the syringe by slowly pulling back on the plunger. In this way you eliminate many of the impurities and adulterants that might otherwise clog the needle. And for obvious reasons you must always, without exception, make absolutely sure that the syringe comes directly from its sealed package. You must see it done before your very eyes. You must never take anyone's word.

I'm in the process of heating up the heroin when Eddie's girlfriend stumbles out of the bedroom in her flannel pajamas and fuzzy pink slippers. She's barely eighteen, and with her mother's permission, as horrific as that may seem since Eddie is my age at forty and a known dope addict, they've been living together for the last six months. That her mother is also a junkie should help to explain though by no means justify her reckless neglect.

I'll call her Crystal, after the drug crystal meth, and she's just woken up, probably having slept through the entire day. Her timing in joining us is as usual uncanny. Like me, she has a sixth sense for when dope is near, and Eddie and I know to keep a close eye on her. Things like rings and watches, and especially drugs, often mysteriously disappear in her presence. It's hard to blame her since she couldn't possibly hold down a job in her condition, let alone attend school. She flops down on the couch with us. Her hair is bleached platinum blond, like Eddie's ex-wife, and she's bone thin from too much heroin, speed, and coke. In the bend of one arm is the swell of a small abscess. Generally they're caused from injecting in or near the same site too often, but sometimes bad junk alone can do it.

"How you doing?" she asks.

"Fine," I say.

"I haven't seen you around in a while."

"Been busy," I say.

Crystal sometimes talks of becoming a cosmetologist. Eddie sometimes talks of opening his own computer repair shop. For now, however, I'm the only one in the room who has a real job, so I have to be careful about how often I get high. And I'm not implying I think of myself as any better than Eddie and Crystal, because I don't. It's just that I have a family. It's just that I've been strung out before, and it's cost me dearly. I believe, like all those who initially start and stop before becoming full-blown addicts, that I'm the exception—that I can use a little here and there for fun, just to relax, without it ever becoming a problem. I do and do not know that I'm lying to myself.

The heroin is bubbling now, turning black, absorbing into the water. Carefully I set the spoon down on the coffee table, unwrap the syringe, and extract the dark liquid into it. Because it's easy to miss the vein or go right through it, because it can make for a bloody mess, even causing the collapse of that vein, including those in the arms, neck, legs, between fingers and toes, I stick it in the middle deltoid of my shoulder. It feels like a mosquito bite. The needle is so thin you hardly notice it piercing your skin, and over the years I've come to like it, the sting, knowing the promise of euphoria is right at the other end.

Where the high from an intravenous injection is almost instantaneous, the intramuscular shot takes fifteen, maybe twenty seconds to hit and it doesn't come over you quite as powerfully. In this narrow span of time, Crystal reaches across me for the other chunk of heroin I left on the coffee table.

"You mind?" she says.

"Help yourself," I say.

She looks to Eddie for approval.

"Baby," he says, "you really need to slow down."

"And you don't?"

I feel it first in the body, a warming from deep inside, filling my chest, then spreading out into my legs and arms. It comes in waves, this sweeping warmth, and as it seeps into the mind all my worries, all my problems and concerns, immediately disappear. Heroin is the most seductive of the narcotics, bringing calm where there is anguish, ease where there is discomfort, and pain, physical or mental, gives way to peace and serenity. The heart slows. Breathing becomes shallow. The mind, emptied of life's clutter, falls into a state of quiet. I feel it pulling me deeper, pulling me under, as if I'm collapsing into myself. In a minute, when the rush levels off, I'm drifting somewhere between wakefulness and dream.

This is the destination.

This is where the outside world ceases to exist and I am as free of it as the dead.

Crystal has found a vein between her toes, though it's taken her a few sticks, and there's blood running down both sides of her ankle. As the rush hits her, as she falls back onto the couch, Eddie hurries to the kitchen and returns with a roll of paper towels and starts cleaning her up. And he does it tenderly. Like a lover. Like a father. I wonder if it's really about her having nowhere else to go. I wonder if it's because she has no real family. I was told her stepfather repeatedly molested her since the age of nine.

For a while, we all just ride the high. Although I'm stoned, I'm still capable enough of understanding what's going on around me. I'm still capable enough of seeing and hearing clearly, and I watch Crystal sit up. I watch her, as if in slow motion, reach for the pack of Marlboros on the coffee table, shake one out and place it between her lips. Before she can light it her chin drops to her chest, and then, as if she were about to fall asleep, she jerks awake. This is called The Nods. Remarkably, the unlit cigarette hasn't slipped from her mouth.

"I don't feel so good," she says.

"Don't throw up here," Eddie says.

Rising slowly from the couch, holding her stomach in her hands, she weaves her way across the room. By now, Eddie has worked up a sweat from cleaning up her blood and to calm himself he depresses the plunger of the syringe hanging from his shoulder, the one containing the dark fluid. Down the hall in the bathroom we hear Crystal retching.

"She gets sick every time," Eddie says. "Never fucking fails."

Even some of the most practiced addicts are cursed with this malady, but it doesn't stop them from using. Once the stomach is emptied, you're clear again to enjoy the heroin high, and further injections, so long as they're not spaced too far apart, don't typically trigger the same loathsome reaction. She takes her place again on the couch. I can smell the peppermint flavored toothpaste she used to wash out her mouth.

"How's your wife," she says in a dreamy, far away kind of voice.

"Good," I say, "though she wouldn't be too happy knowing I'm here."

"I hope you don't get in trouble."

Of course I'll get in trouble if my wife finds out. But she's visiting relatives in Tennessee, and my sons are spending the week with their grandparents in Northern California. Tonight I have no schedule. Tonight I am accountable to no one, and frequently these are the occasions when I mess up, when I'm alone and the bright idea to get wasted suddenly pops into my head.

"She's so pretty," she says in that dream voice again.

By no means is this Crystal's way of flirting with me.

She's genuinely interested in my wife. At every A.A. meeting, when we were all still clean and sober, and whenever my wife accompanied me in support, which she did often, Crystal would stare at her from across the room. And there was something desperate about it. Something sad. Something pathetic. It was the way a young girl stares admiringly at a beautiful older woman, the one the girl wishes to be like, the one she might've hoped to have had for a mother. And because she did not, because she lacks the confidence and self-esteem that is every child's birthright, because narcotics steal any fleeting hope of a better life, Crystal trades, as her mother still trades, on her sexuality.

"Can I have a little more?"

Her request for dope is directed at Eddie this time, but he ignores her. He has made a fist of his left hand. Even with the syringes still dangling from his shoulders, he is searching for a vein between his fingers, to mainline, to get the most powerful, immediate rush possible, and he cannot be interrupted. Again and again he misses, extracts the needle, then jabs it back in. Blood fills the crevices between his fingers and curls around his wrist and drips onto the carpet. Crystal reaches for another chunk of heroin, a piece he set aside from the scale, because it tipped the beam over a gram, and soon she too is looking for a vein, again between her toes. Soon she too is bleeding.

I press my hands together.

So they can see better, they kneel on the floor before the table lamp. They search, and in the dim light, heads bowed and blood leaking from their wounds, it looks to me as if we are all engaged in some grotesque act of prayer. Though I've seen worse, junkies stabbing into an oozing abscess, or sticking the jugular, even I'm repulsed by all the blood.

"Eddie, man," I say. "Forget it. You're making a big mess."

But he ignores me, as he did Crystal, that or he's too obsessed with finding and hitting a vein to hear me. Finally he succeeds. Crystal isn't far behind. Their eyes roll back into their heads and then their lids slowly close. They're far away now, in a fine place where no one can reach them. Neither will miss me. Neither will notice when I gather up what I came for and leave.

RELAPSE

My head is full of pictures. A pillow heavy with blood and teeming with maggots. My sister's cracked skull on the concrete banks of the Los Angeles River. Holding my father's cold dead hand. My head has been full of these pictures and others like them for years, and for years I've rarely slept more than four or five hours a night.

I am sitting at the kitchen table with my family, two months after the needless death of my ex-wife, and there is a void. An insidious quiet surrounding her absence. We are all in mourning, still dazed and shell-shocked by her sudden passing, when I have what is commonly referred to as a breakdown. In the field of psychiatry, it is generalized as a psychotic episode. For me, it is simply the overwhelming compulsion to stop the picture-making mechanism.

Dinner is lamb chops, baked potato, fresh green beans.

It is a good meal made by a good wife for good children.

But the man at this table is neither a good father or good husband. He is and has been for most of his life mentally ill without knowing it. Also, he is and has been for most of his life an alcoholic. He is a black-out drinker. He drinks to erase the memory, to wash the slate clean of all thought, but as the drinking progresses, so does the sickness of the mind, and the gruesome pictures, instead of fading, become increasingly vivid. The decision is and is not my own, for I am no more capable of rational thought than I am controlling the scenes and images that replay themselves over and over in an endless loop in my head. I don't yet have the clarity of mind to see the act as the ultimate in selfishness. I don't yet have the clarity of mind to realize that my life is not solely my own.

I'm a chronic relapser, putting together six or seven months of sobriety here, three or four months there, and twice I've made it over a full year. Before Heidi's death, I almost had another three hundred and sixty-five days clean and sober, just a few weeks shy of taking my third one year chip. Fact is, I'm back to my old ways again, drinking heavily and daily for over two months now when I push the dinner plate away from me and rise from the table.

I go to the kitchen drawer.

I take out the box of garbage bags. Paula and the boys stare at me. Nate is six. Logan is twelve. Andy, my oldest, is out with his girlfriend, but he will be home soon enough to intervene.

"What're you doing?" she says.

"Nothing," I say.

Though I've consumed a fifth of Smirnoff over the course of the afternoon, I don't feel drunk, and I walk steadily up the stairs to our bedroom. I grab my wallet off the dresser so I can be identified. I grab my keys and go to the closet. In the corner, behind the shirts and pants my wife has washed and neatly hung for me, are several long-range hunting rifles I inherited from my father, but I choose his Remington twelve gauge. I am a believer in the definitive power of the shotgun.

I have no intention of using it here. Even in my deeply troubled state, I would never impress on the memory of those I love what is permanently etched in mine. Instead, the plan is to drive out into the forest near our home, double-line two garbage bags and pull them over my head before placing the barrel in my mouth. My brother did it this way, only with a .38, but he lacked the consideration, or maybe it's foresight, of first covering himself. Cleaning up the aftermath is one of the pictures I can't shake. I reach for the box of shells as Paula comes up behind me.

"Give me those."

She grabs my hand. The flimsy cardboard splits open and shells scatter across the carpet.

"Get out of here," I say.

I stoop to pick up the shells and she kicks them away. But I manage to hang onto one and that's all I need. My rifles are propped up in the corner of the closet and I have to push aside my clothes to get at them. Before I can take the twelve gauge, however, she's scratching at my back, my arms, digging her nails in deep. Then Andy and Logan are on me, and together with Paula they're able to corral me outside and into the car. I don't recall what was said in the process, though I'm sure there had to be plenty of shouting. I don't see myself going peacefully.

On this night, I find myself in the front seat of Paula's car. Logan sits in the back but he has his arms wrapped around me from behind. Andy, I'm later told, stays home to look after his littlest brother. The destination is Ward B of the San Bernardino County Jail. Ward B is the way-station for the 5150's, California Welfare and Institution Code for an involuntary psychiatric hold, and a part of me believes this is where I belong. But another part, a stronger part, resists. I've heard about this place. I've had friends from A.A. and N.A. who have wound up here and their stories are ugly. Paula has gone to open meetings, when they allow in non-alcoholics, and this is where she also learns about Ward B.

"I hope you realize what you're doing to me."

"I just want you safe until you can see a doctor."

"This place is for crazy people. The real crazies, the drooling, the catatonic. I'm messed up," I say. "I admit I'm messed up. But I'm not crazy."

"Just calm down," she says.

"Pull over."

But she doesn't. I feel Logan tighten his arms around my chest. He is a physically strong boy but I am a physically strong man, and as Paula slows to turn onto Rialto Street on the outskirts of San Bernardino, as we're approaching our destination, I break my son's grip. I open the door and jump.

He opens the back door and follows.

My adrenalin is pumping, and with it my mood changes from one of fear and confusion to elation. Every nerve is alive. My senses are preternaturally keen. I run across an open field, Logan at my heels, and I smell the mustard weed, sweet and pungent. I feel the dampness of the tall grass brushing against my pant legs and the rhythm of my strides seem in perfect sync with my breathing. The skin on my arms is prickly. It's a rush heightened further still with the knowledge that I'm soon to be hunted. Paula, I'm certain, will continue on to the police station and tell them her husband has flipped and is running the streets with her twelve-year-old stepson.

A decent father, and a mentally stable one, would never put his child in harm's way, but I'm neither a decent father nor a stable one. Although it has never been my intent to hurt my son, I've been sabotaging his childhood, and that of his brothers, long before this night. Worrying, damaging, terrorizing those closest to us, intentionally or not, is what alcoholics, addicts, and the mentally ill do best. Careening into a depression after a long run of sleeplessness, drug induced or not, I can go from being a kind and gentle man to a raving bastard in a matter of seconds.

For now, however, I am focused only on my freedom, and in the distance, maybe three or four miles away, I see the big bright red letters of the Hilton in downtown San Bernardino. Logan and I slow to a walk. We're breathing heavily.

I point to the sign.

"If we make it there," I say, "we can lay low until tomorrow. We'll figure things out then. Right now we have to watch out for cops. Can you do that? Be my lookout?"

Logan nods.

Though I am sure he is scared for and of me, though I am sure he would much rather I seek help than run from it, he is loving and loyal. And when I'm sober we have moments when we really connect, father to son. He knows this, and after the last court battle with Heidi, when I could pass a drug test, the right to have my kids on the weekends was returned to me. But tensions rose between Logan and his mother. She would tell our children bad things about me. Logan, I understand, grew tired of hearing it, and once, when he stuck up for me, it enraged her. She struck him again and again until he struck back and blackened her eye. That's when she allowed him a choice: to live with me or her.

He chose his father.

So Logan is my ally. So Logan is a confused young boy used to obeying his father rather than confronting him. So Logan becomes my partner in this getaway and a hostage to my madness. That he recently suffered the sudden loss of his mother and is already in great pain and anguish does not, at least for the moment, enter my mind. I am and am not unaware that I'm inflicting further psychological damage on him. I am grateful that scrapes and bruises are his only injuries from jumping out of the car. We are both lucky.

The glowing Hilton sign is a beacon in the night. Getting there, however, is a treacherous adventure through the gang lands and ghettos of a city best known as the meth capital of our nation. Crack and heroin and prostitution belong to the mix, and the neighborhoods are divided by turf and race. Black and brown. That my son and I are white means some view us as potential customers, or enemies, and others as easy muggings. One or two might enjoy killing us for sport. My son is rightfully scared of the lanky young boys loitering on the corners, waiting for a car to pull up and do business, and as we're crossing a street he witnesses a transaction.

"Dad," he says. "That guy just gave him some money and the other guy gave him a matchbook."

"Don't stare," I say.

"But I think it's a drug deal."

"We mind our business," I say, "They mind theirs.

Simple as that."

Judging by his reaction, it's likely the first deal he's ever witnessed, and being the son of a father who's spent the better part of his life under the influence, I'm grateful he's shocked by it—that this isn't a common occurrence in his life, as it has been in mine. I hope none of my sons follow in my footsteps, that the cycle of addiction stops with me, but I fear the worst. They have seen too much. They have been hurt too deeply, too often, and that pain can well up with a vengeance later in life, warping and destroying everything.

Because I know these parts well, because I've scored if not in this exact location then somewhere nearby, I'm not so much nervous as alert. I'm comfortable here—in my element. The underworld of dope and sin. But I also know not to trust these kids, that some have no conscience or morals and will turn on you quick, so I pack with a load in the chamber when I score around here. It's a last resort, buying dope off the street, and not necessarily for the danger, but because the stuff is usually heavily cut, its potency diluted.

Two hookers linger at the end of the block. One wears fishnet stockings and heels. The other is in short-shorts and a T-shirt tied in a knot under her breasts. They're past their prime, road worn and strung out.

"Hey," one says.

"Hey," I say.

"What's your hurry?" she says. "Come here, talk to me."

"Later," I say.

They're standing under a street lamp, and I see her make a face as if she's hurt, a cute sort of pout. That I'm with my boy doesn't seem to matter. Some tricks must just make their kids wait. Maybe I'm a mental case, but I'm not that fucked up. Despite evidence to the contrary, in intervals I can and have been a decent father, coaching my sons in freestyle wrestling, weight lifting, taking them camping and fishing, telling them bed time stories, kissing them good night, teaching them manners, and reminding them how much I love them. All this pales, however, in the morass of shame and guilt associated with my drinking and drugging and the attendant madness. To love without hurting them is a delicate balancing act.

When we're down the block, out of earshot, Logan looks at me.

"Those were whores."

"Working girls," I say. "Or prostitutes. Whore is a dirty word. They're just doing a job, trying to get by like everybody else."

"Cops," Logan says.

"What?"

"Cops."

"Where?"

He points.

A cruiser approaches from up the street. I can make out the rack of lights on top. We're just about to cross an overpass, there's a dry creek below, and we jump the railing and hide behind the concrete pilings beneath it. Someone has built a shelter here made of cardboard and plywood, and we squat beside it in the dark. Though my adrenalin is still pumping, the elation has given way to fear again.

"Think they saw us?"

I'm breathing hard and I try to steady it.

"I don't know," I say.

Logan looks at the cardboard and plywood shelter. He's uneasy, though not because of the cops. There's a rustling, the crinkle of newspaper, from behind the make-shift walls.

"I think someone's in there."

"We mind our business," I say, "whoever's living there minds his. I'm sure he doesn't want trouble any more than we do."

Above a car passes, probably the cruiser, and we wait until the sound of the engine fades before we continue on our way. The Hilton sign is like a mirage. It looks like it's only a couple of blocks away, but it's still a good mile or so. We don't run. We walk but we walk quickly, vigilant, hyper-aware, constantly looking around us. It must be near ten p.m., and at this time of night the streets are mostly empty except for a few homeless and every now and then a hooker or a kid or two, high maybe, with nowhere else to go.

Finally, without further incident, we reach the hotel. We're exhausted, but I feel my spirits lift because I know there's a drink waiting just for me at the hotel bar. There will also be a room with two double beds and fresh clean sheets and a nice warm shower. There will be a TV, and for a night cap or two, a mini-fridge stocked with little bottles of vodka and whiskey.

The electric doors slide open for us and we head through the high-ceiled lobby to the reception desk. I brush my hands through my hair, trying, impossibly, to make myself appear presentable. I'm sure we both look a little beaten and scruffy, but for what the clerk knows we've been traveling all day and night.

"My son and I'd like a room for the night," I say. "One with two double beds."

"Do you have reservations?"

"No."

"Give me a second."

The Hilton is the last decent hotel in downtown San Bernardino, and because of the area, how it changed from a city of relative prosperity to a ghetto when the local military bases were shut down and the enlistees' apartments were turned into Section 8 housing, I know they have plenty of rooms.

I look at Logan.

"Let's do it in style. It's been a hell of a night." I look at the clerk. "Give us a suite with a mini-bar," I say. "Top floor. By the way," I say, "how late does the lounge stay open? The boy's starving and I wouldn't mind a drink."

The clerk glances at his watch.

"It's open until midnight. We stop serving dinner at ten but you can still order appetizers. Any luggage tonight, Mr. Brown?"

"No," I say. "We just need some sleep and food before we hit the road again tomorrow."

But first things first. I need a few drinks before we check into our room, so we head straight for the lounge. The place is dead. Aside from the bartender, we're the only ones there, and he lets my son sit next to me up at the bar. Logan looks at the appetizer menu.

"I'll have a double Smirnoff on the rocks. Son," I say, "what would you like?"

"A coke," he says.

"You ever try a Shirley Temple?"

"Huh?"

"Sometimes they call them a Roy Rogers. This is back in the day."

The bartender is from my generation and knows what I'm talking about.

"You'll love it," he says, "and if you don't, we'll get you a regular coke. Anything to eat?"

"Buffalo wings."

I smile at my son.

"Make that two orders," I say. "He's a growing boy."

Buffalo wings are one of his favorite foods, and on many occasions I've made them for dinner with him in mind. His brothers like them too, and I take a special pleasure in cooking for the boys. Regrettably, I usually drink as I prepare the meal, and I'm too drunk to enjoy it with them when I serve up the plates.

After a couple rounds of double shots, my head begins to clear and my hands are steady again. Leaving the bartender a generous tip for letting Logan sit at the bar with me, and for pouring me heavy drinks, we go to our suite. To a kid who hasn't stayed in many hotels, this is a big deal, and despite the circumstances, he's thrilled and awed by the orderliness, the luxury, the spaciousness.

"Dad," he says, flipping the light on in the bathroom, "this is bigger than our kitchen." He hurries to the window and pulls back the drapes. "Check out this view. You can see the whole city from here."

I'm pleased he's excited, but the ease and comfort that came with drinking the vodka is fleeting, and my mood suddenly changes to paranoia. How could I be so stupid? I paid the clerk with a credit card, and if the cops are after me, as I'm certain they are, they could phone the different hotels to see if any James Brown checked in tonight. I know Paula is worried about Logan. I know Paula is worried about me and went to the police. What I don't know is how thoroughly they intend to check out her complaint.

I step behind the sofa.

"Help me move this?"

"What?"

"I need you to push while I pull."

Together we drag the sofa against the door. It just fits, not an inch to spare on either side of the hallway.

Logan is the voice is reason.

"This because of the cops?"

"Yeah."

"I don't think it'll stop them. If they want to get in, they'll get in."

"I'm sure you're right, but we'll give the bastards a run for their money. C'mon," I say, "help me with this chair."

Onto the sofa we wrestle its two matching chairs and a writing desk. It'll take some serious shoving to get this door open. Perched at the top is the coffee table, which will be the first thing to fall, alerting us, when they try to bust through. I'm proud of my ingenuity. I'm proud of my foresight. Though in hindsight I recognize my behavior as bizarre, at the time it seemed perfectly normal to me. The hunted are desperate, and I was, to my mind, the hunted.

I stand back and look at our handiwork.

"Now let the fuckers get in. Either way," I say, "at least we'll sleep a little easier tonight."

But when it's time to turn off the lights and slip under the covers, when my eyes finally close, and only then out of sheer exhaustion, I'm visited again by my first and earliest memory of death.

In it, I'm five or six years old, playing along the concrete pathway of the house next door to ours in San Jose.

There is a window on the second floor of this house. The window is open. The back of a couch is pushed against it.

I look up.

Why, I don't know. Maybe I hear something. Maybe it's instinct. But I see the baby perfectly, its little bald head, and I remember initially being more puzzled than alarmed.

In the remembering, the fall always occurs in slow motion. In real time, it takes only a second, and I hear clearly the slap of its newly formed skull, still soft, makes against the pavement. A thin stream of blood leaks from the temple. I am only several feet away.

The mother leans out the window.

"My baby," she says. "My baby."

The slap of the skull echoes through the years, and I attribute it to age, to becoming a parent myself and realizing that no agony can be greater than the death of one's child.

The thing is, I could've saved that baby.

The thing is, I could've put my arms out to break the fall. But I just stand there, and sometimes, when I think too long about it, I see one of my boy's faces in that baby. When you can prevent a death but do nothing, you might as well consider yourself an accomplice to murder. Shock. Paralysis. Cowardice. These are no excuses for failing to act.

Same place. Same year.

I'm playing outside when a little black girl from down the block, just learning to ride her bike, rolls down her driveway into the street with a big smile on her face just as a car speeds by. As she lays dying in the street, I am amazed at the length of her intestines stretching ten, maybe fifteen feet across the asphalt, and when the ambulance arrives the attendant scoops them up and puts them back inside her, gravel and all. Her last words are "Mommy...mommy," and like the baby that falls from the window she too sometimes visits me at night.

I wish I would've seen the car coming.

I am awake now.

The red glowing numbers of the clock on the bedstand read 4:06 a.m. Oddly, though I've only slept a few hours, I'm completely rejuvenated. I'm full of energy. I feel great. No hangover. No lingering memories of death.

I'm ready for breakfast, the newspaper, a quick stroll around the block. But Logan is still fast asleep, and I realize it's not likely I'll find a restaurant open at this hour. So I wait it out, at least until 5:15, when I take a long hot shower. By 5:45 I'm clean and dressed, and it occurs to me that I should call home and let Paula know we're okay. Then I'll wake Logan. He can shower. Then we can get breakfast.

I pick up the hotel phone and dial nine for an outside number. Of course I'm embarrassed about it all. Of course I'd rather not even call. But I know I have to, that I owe her that much. Paula picks up on the first ring, her voice groggy, though not for long.

"Jim?"

"Yeah."

"Where are you? What happened to Logan? Is he hurt? Are you okay?

"Take it easy," I say. "He's fine. We're both fine, just a little scraped up."

"Let me talk to him. I want to talk to him."

"He's still sleeping and I don't want to wake him."

"Christ, Jim, your son, your own son, he could've killed himself. What the hell were you thinking jumping out of the car?" She pauses. "Where are you?"

But I'm not sure I want to give up my location without some assurance that jails or institutions aren't a part of the equation.

"You won't call the cops?"

"No."

"Promise?"

"I promise," she says. "I just want you both back home.

I've been up worrying all night. Orlando will come and get you."

Orlando and I have been friends for close to thirty years. He's seen me in good times. He's nursed me through the bad times and tolerated too many drunken late night phone calls. But this is absolutely not the time to involve him.

"His mother is in the hospital," I say. "She's dying, you know. The last thing he needs is you heaping my shit on him."

"Just tell me where you are."

I didn't figure on her calling Orlando, though I probably should have, since in many ways he knows me better than she does and she needs his support and advice. I don't have any game plan, either, other than to return home peacefully and see if we can't put this mess behind us. I don't know any other way to handle it. I don't know if there is another way. All I can do is apologize and swear never to do it again. Unfortunately, the promises of this alcoholic are empty, for they are the promises of a person who, despite his best efforts, despite his best intentions, can't control his drinking. It's as if I have a mental blank spot where I'm unable, as the Big Book says, to recall "with sufficient force the memory of the suffering and humiliation of even a week or a month ago."

"The Hilton."

"Downtown?"

"On E Street," I say. "But Logan and I are going out to breakfast first. Are you still taking Nate to his game this morning?"

"Of course," she says. "There's no reason he should suffer because of you."

I agree fully. I wouldn't want it any other way. The world does not, contrary to how I may act or what I might like to believe, revolve around me. We hang up shortly after that and not two minutes later the phone rings. It's Orlando, and the conversation is short. I tell him to meet me at the hotel restaurant in an hour.

"Bullshit," he says. "I'm leaving now and you better not go anywhere."

At breakfast, it's hard to look my friend in the eye. I know Paula has told him everything. The suicide threat. Jumping from a moving car. My shame and guilt and self-loathing is only intensified by Orlando's presence. He knows I know better. I know I know better. I blame so much of it on the alcohol because I'm a different and better person sober, but once I start drinking I can't stop, and because I can't stop I despise myself for what I see as a fatal defect of character.

"You've quit before," Orlando tells me. "You can quit again. I love you, motherfucker. I don't want to have to bury you."

"Dad?" Logan says.

"What?"

"Listen to him. Please. He's telling you the truth."

My boy, after all I've put him through, has yet to break. But finally all he's been holding inside rises to the surface and he begins to cry. Seeing his tears spark my own. A family of four and several others in the neighboring booths are eating and at least pretending to pay us no mind.

I signed Nate up for soccer to keep him involved and busy and in shape for when wrestling season gears up. He plays for the Wolverines. The little kids' soccer games start at nine on Saturday mornings. It's about nine thirty when we make it up the mountain, and though I've already missed the first half, I'm counting on catching the tail end of the game. We approach the street where we're supposed to turn.

"Make a left up there," I say.

But Orlando continues on straight.

"Where you going?"

"Let's swing by your place first."

"But I'll miss the game."

Orlando is silent. He's up to something, though what I don't know. I'm sure I ask but I don't remember him answering.

The next memory takes me directly to my house when I step into the living room and discover what under ordinary circumstances would've seemed like a surprise birthday party. Only it's no birthday party. Art, another one of my best friends, is here, and he's brought along a buddy I've met only once before. They're both screenwriters who drove two hours in from L.A. Both belong to A.A., though their drugs of choice are pharmaceutical. My next-door neighbor is also present, a tough old man with sinewy muscles and a faded tattoo of a naked woman on his forearm. He's in A.A., too, seventeen years clean and sober.

They're all seated at the dining room table and rise when I come in. My wife, who I am not altogether pleased with at this moment, steps toward me. At thirty-one, fifteen years younger than me, she is staunchly resolute. I was once her professor. She was once my student. Now, apparently, those roles are reversed.

"Your friends," she says, "they're here to talk to you."

* * *

Obsession, like mania, is a blessing and a curse. Properly channeled I am able to focus on my writing, my teaching duties, or physical exercise with what some may consider a frightening intensity. An ordinary chore that might take the average person an hour to complete, I can do in half the time or less. But the Law of Gravity is inescapable: What goes up, must come down, and the higher you go, the harder you fall.

Elation and energy become depression and lethargy. In the crash, certain thoughts and images get stuck in my head and I can't get them out by simply trying to think of something else. Distractions don't work. Willing them away is futile. Once they're locked in, and it can happen in a flash, I'm at the mercy of my own mind. The What-If Factor burrows itself deep into my consciousness, and fully awake or deep in dream, the most recent guest in my catalogue of guilt and psychosis is Heidi.

Although we are divorced several years before she passes, although she tried to take my children from me, in the face of her death absolutely none of this matters. And whether it's rational or not, I blame myself. My reasoning works like this:

If we hadn't divorced, she never would've met this other man, who wanted a baby by her, and so at the age of forty-three she never would've had her tubes untied and gotten pregnant.

If we hadn't divorced, there would be no complications due to her pregnancy.

The baby is born fine.

But ten days later, if we hadn't divorced, the doctors wouldn't have misdiagnosed her complaints of gaining weight rather than losing it after delivery as post-partum depression.

If, after further complaints of shortness of breath and swelling of the limbs, the doctors hadn't again misdiagnosed her ailment as a pulmonary embolism and put her on blood thinners, the boys would still have their mother. If, when the doctor draws a sample of fluid from her lungs, he hadn't punctured an artery, she would not have internally bled to death.

The bleeding can't be stemmed because of the blood thinners they'd given her, and if when Andy and I followed her ambulance down the mountain to Saint Bernardine's Hospital in the ghetto on the night she was admitted, if she and the other man would've just listened when we insisted she transfer to a better hospital only a few miles away, maybe she'd still be here. Our marriage wasn't always troubled. There were good years, especially in the beginning, and just because we divorced doesn't mean I stopped caring for her. Heidi gave me the greatest gift of all, three beautiful boys, and for this I will always love her.

Nonetheless, our break-up set into motion a series of events that lead to her death, and because I initiate the split, I feel accountable. The hardest thing I've ever had to do is sit my boys down three days after Heidi is put on life support.

"Your mother," I say, "may not be coming home."

I say it with absolutely no intention of crushing whatever hope they may hold. I am trying only to soften the blow of what I have come to see as inevitable. I watched my father die on those fucking ventilators, tube stuffed down his throat, unable to talk, answering yes and no to questions by squeezing my hand until finally there is no strength left for even the slightest response.

I was there to the end with Heidi as well. She goes the same way, the hand slowly weakening when they take her off life support, and now, myself in a hospital for those of troubled minds, addicts, and alcoholics, I relive her last days as I ride out the first throes of withdrawal. I shake. I sweat. I'm sick to my stomach. The nurses initially treat me with strong doses of Valium, and because my blood pressure rockets dangerously high, I'm given Clonidine, a powerful antihypertensive, to reduce the possibility of stroke. During this time, I spend eighteen to twenty hours a day in bed, in and out of consciousness.

The doctors and nurses are doing what they can to minimize the misery of detox and withdrawal, and I appreciate their good intentions, but knocking me out can be dangerous.

Sometimes I need to wake up, and taking away that capability can leave me stranded in the coldest of dark waters. My brother and sister are the most frequent visitors in my dreams and rank at the top of my What-If Factor column.

What *could* I have done to save them?

What *should* I have done to save them?

And why didn't I see their suicides coming, especially Marilyn's, since I had knowledge of the signs and symptoms from our brother's?

My experience, and what I've learned from friends who've found themselves in my position, is that rehabs are generally pretty much the same. Most are built around the Twelve Steps of Alcoholics Anonymous, distinguished more by class and money than methodology. There is rehab for the poor and indigent and the accommodations reflect it. There is rehab for the rich—elegant housing with private rooms with views of the Pacific or the Hollywood Hills, places made famous by their celebrity clientele whose careers often take precedent over sobriety.

Then there are Behavioral Modification Centers, like the one I'm at, that tackle the psych cases alongside alcoholics and addicts or any combination thereof. The building, its layout and design, is no different than a hospital with its orderlies and registered nurses and drab rooms with curtain partitions. Instead of medical doctors, however, you have psychiatrists who come around to your room periodically, make notes on your chart and chat a few minutes before moving on to the next patient.

Since I'm out of it the first week, I don't do much talking. But by the fifth or sixth day, they begin weaning me off the

Valium and slowly reduce my dosage of Clonidine as my blood pressure stabilizes. The routine, once I'm on my feet again, revolves around group counseling, lectures, and films on the damaging effects of alcohol and drugs on the mind and body, regular attendance at an on-premise Alcoholics Anonymous or Narcotics Anonymous meeting, and daily one-on-one sessions with a psychiatrist or drug and alcohol counselor.

Tonight, after dinner, I go to an A.A. meeting held in the recreation room at the hospital. The leader is one of the head counselors, known among the staff and patients as Tradition Dale for his strict and unwavering allegiance to the principles of Alcoholics Anonymous. One glance at his face and you know he spent the better part of his fifty odd years drinking heavily before sobering up. He has the telltale bulbous nose, and across it runs a thin spiderlike pattern of broken blood vessels.

"How many days you got, Jim?"

"I think about twelve now," I say. "Since I was admitted."

"You *think* or you *know*? You need an exact sobriety date," he says. "You need to keep a perfect count. I have 3,672 days clean and sober, and God willing, tomorrow it'll be 3,673."

Tradition Dale is big on God, which has always been the single greatest stumbling block for me in embracing A.A. I've been told time after time that I need a Higher Power to stay sober and that this Higher Power can be anything I want it to be, from a doorknob to the group itself. Fake it until you make it. That's one of their major slogans, and I have trouble with its line of reasoning—lie to yourself until you're convinced the lie is true.

People shuffle in shortly before the meeting starts.

It's a small group, fifteen or so, most of them patients here, others visitors from the surrounding communities. The fold-out chairs are arranged in a circle. Tradition Dale passes around laminated placards, one with the Twelve Traditions of A.A., another taken from Chapter Five of the Big Book containing the Twelve Steps, and a third entitled "The Promises," which has everything to do with how staying sober will remarkably improve the quality of your life. The first two are read aloud as a kind of preamble before the sharing of personal stories begins. "The Promises" are saved for the end, so as to put a spin of optimism to even the darkest of meetings.

And they can get pretty dark.

One of the greatest realizations to come from A.A., at least for myself, is learning that there are plenty of others out there just as screwed up and troubled as me. Some even more so. It's no consolation, but it does give me a perverse sense of belonging in a world that by and large considers people like me moral degenerates when in truth we are profoundly ill, our so-called will power nonexistent. No one is immune to addiction, and the addict, like the alcoholic, does not set out to hurt others. The drug, the bottle, immobilizes all sense of self-control, self-respect, self-esteem, and rational judgment.

After the preambles are read, Tradition Dale calls on one of the group to share. She's a young woman with a bony, angular forehead and sunken cheeks. She looks fragile, both physically and emotionally, as if at any moment she might burst into tears. I've seen her in other meetings, but she's not a patient here.

"I'm Gloria," she says, "and I'm a grateful alcoholic.

I'm glad I've been asked to share because I'm going through hell right now. It's been a year since Charlie died, and

I know they say it's supposed to get easier with time, but for me it only gets worse." She looks around the group, and I feel myself identifying with her. "I don't think I'll ever be the same. He was always happy to see me when I came home, always there to cheer me up when I was feeling blue. You couldn't ask for a better companion. We went everywhere together and now he's gone and I still can't believe it. Last night, I woke up thinking he was in bed with me, but when I reached over to pet him he wasn't there. The sheets were cold." She pauses. She stares down at the floor.

"My friends tell me I should get a puppy, but it wouldn't be fair to Charlie. I mean, it's just not right, especially so soon."

A teenage heroin addict in the chair beside me leans over and whispers in my ear.

"She talking about a *dog*?"

"I think so," I say. "Some people really get attached to their pets."

"I know," he says. "But it's still just a fucking dog."

If addiction has one redeeming value, it's that it doesn't discriminate, crossing all ethnic, economic, and social barriers. In this group we have the teenage heroin addict sitting next to me, a doctor who used to prescribe his own morphine sulfate, a paramedic who couldn't keep his hands out of the emergency med kit, a housewife strung out on wine and Xanax, and a Beverly Hills building contractor hooked on pain meds. Across from me is a thirty-something crackhead who hails from that easy going city of Compton, its resident Crips and their beloved brethren, the Bloods. He has prison tats covering both arms, and on his neck, in fancy script, is the name LaKesha. Dale calls on him.

"I'm Ronnie," he says, "and I'm a dope fiend and a drunk. My father was a dope fiend and a drunk. My mother was a dope fiend and a drunk. My two brothers are dope fiends and drunks. Getting wasted in my family is a way of *life*." This guy doesn't so much talk as shout, and he can't seem to sit still. I've heard him share before and I like his passion. I like that he's a little over the top, since the rest of us are typically more subdued. "Normal, for me, is being fucked up. Normal, for me, is getting sick on Thunderbird. Normal, for me, is spending every cent I make on rock. Can't pay the rent, no problem. Just do another rock. Electric company turns off the power, no problem. Just do another rock. And when the money's gone, and the dopeman don't answer the door, you do what got to do. Pimp your old lady. Pimp your daughter. Rob some punk, split open his motherfucking head. Ain't nothing stop me from getting the rock till the police send my sorry black ass back to prison where it belong. Who all here would go that far?" He looks around the group, trying to register his effect on us. He wants to shock. He wants, I think, to show us that his addiction is somehow stronger and more real than ours because it comes from the street. "That's the monkey," he says. "That's the jones. Let me tell you all something and then I'll shut the fuck up. When I get out of here, first thing I'll do is fire up that crack pipe. And you know what? Listen now," he says, "because this is the kicker. It won't be 'cause I want to. I mean, I know rock fucks up my life. I know it takes me back to prison. Every time. But I'll do it anyway. I'll do it because of one thing. Because," he says, "it's who I am."

On that hopeful note, Tradition Dale calls on the doctor to speak, the morphine addict, who confesses to having intercourse with underage female patients after he's knocked them out with an anesthetic. After that, it's the building contractor whose foray into addiction started with a minor back injury and a generous prescription for Oxycontin and Loratab, both synthetic narcotics on par with morphine and heroin.

Communality and openness have never come easily to me. By nature I'm a cynic and somewhat introverted, and I hold any public display of camaraderie suspect. I'll accept as truth man's darker nature far more readily than I will his good heartedness. Sober only for a short while, I'm realizing that I am sick. I'm in the right place for help. I know I belong here. I'm no different or better than anyone in the group, excluding the child molester, and when I leave the meeting that evening I somehow feel uplifted. I feel, somehow, that I'm making progress, and now that I've detoxed I'd like to go home. I need to be there for my boys, but since I'm still considered a danger to myself and possibly others, they won't just let me leave on my own accord. Scaling the fence, breaking out, also isn't the brightest idea, given that the hospital is located in the desert, miles from the main highway. In the summer, temperatures reach 110, often higher, and in the winter come the powerful winds that darken the sky with clouds of dust and debris. Except for the indigenous rattlers and lizards, life here stops where the water ends, and it's that borderline, on the cusp of survival and devastation, that strikes me as the perfect place for the alcoholic and the addict who spend their days constantly navigating between the two.

Judging from the first couple of sessions with the psychiatrist, I think I've convinced him that I'm much better now. I've done close to a complete one-eighty in record time. Bottom line: I'm nothing more than your regular, run-of-the-mill alcoholic who simply lost control one night and threatened to kill himself.

"I know it sounds bad," I say, "but really, honestly, I didn't mean it."

For the most part, I'm straight up with the man. I am not, however, aware of the many things my wife has told him, and now he wants to have a meeting with both of us. Several days later, Paula arrives at his office with a cup of Starbucks. I'm in sweatpants and a T-shirt, standard garb for the patients. I don't know why it is, but when I haven't seen her for a few days, she always looks more beautiful than ever.

The doctor is blunt.

"I understand your brother and sister were both alcoholics. I understand they both killed themselves. What makes you think your situation is any less dire."

"Because it isn't."

"That's not a good enough answer. Paula tells me you have nightmares."

"Occasionally," I say, "like anybody else."

"Oh come off it," she says, "you haven't slept a full night since I've known you. He dreams about maggots under his brother's pillow and thinks there's maggots under his." She's referring to what I regret having shared with her about finding maggots under the pillow heavy with my brother's blood. He shot himself in bed. "Sometimes he wakes up crying. Sometimes he wakes up screaming. He's hit me in his sleep, if you can call it sleep. Be honest," she says, "or he can't help us."

The doctor tends to look more at Paula than me as he speaks, and before he makes his diagnosis, he explains to us that the drug of choice from those suffering from bipolar disorder is alcohol. He adds to his verdict the possibility of mild schizophrenia. In short, he's saying I'm really fucked up.

"Like alcoholism," he says, "it's a genetic illness, passed down from one generation to the next. We know this now. The studies are irrefutable. But what we didn't have before, and what we have today, are the better medications to treat it. I'm not saying your alcoholism isn't its own problem now, only that it's exacerbated by your condition and likely to get worse if left untreated. You also suffer from post-traumatic stress disorder."

To accept his diagnosis is to accept that I'm a whole lot sicker than I thought, and though I'm willing to acknowledge my alcoholism, I'm not quick to take on the label of bipolar. I also resent the euphemism of the term, the politically correct vagueness of an illness more aptly described by its symptoms—mood swings from one extreme to the other, from energy and vigor to exhaustion and lethargy, what was formerly coined manic-depression. The doctor recommends Seroquel.

"It usually takes anywhere from a week to ten days for your nervous system to adjust," he says, "but once it does, the side effects should disappear. The main thing is that it'll help you sleep."

Paula sighs in relief.

"Is it a tranquilizer?"

"Not in the typical sense of the word. It's classified as an anti-psychotic, though it does have tranquilizing effects."

Great, I think. So now I'm psychotic.

"I don't know about this," I say.

"He said it'll help you sleep. Why can't you at least try it?"

Believing but not wanting to believe that the doctor may be onto something, coupled with the pressure from my wife, I cave.

The side effects, though temporary, are many. Garbled speech. Short term memory loss. Physical coordination problems. I literally have to think about putting one foot before the other to walk, and when I reach for something, maybe just the lamp switch on the bedstand in my hospital room, or a simple cup of coffee, I need to concentrate on the path along which I want my hand to move. Somehow, and this is not always necessarily for the better, it kills my dreams, and not all my dreams are bad, but for the first time in I don't know how many years I'm able to sleep a full eight hours.

I don't see falling babies.

I don't see maggots and bloody pillows or my sister's body sprawled on the concrete banks of the Los Angeles River, her limbs bent in all the wrong directions. If I do, I don't recall any of it when I wake up. It is an amazing drug that will later play a pivotal role in my achieving long–term sobriety.

For now, however, I remain in this Behavioral Modification Center, and it's nearing ten o'clock, when all patients are supposed to be in bed. The teenage heroin addict pokes his head into my room just minutes after one of the nurses gives me my Seroquel along with a little paper cup full of other pills of unknown origin. I don't even bother asking anymore.

"Phone," he says.

There's a payphone in the hall. Whenever it rings, and whoever happens to hear it, that person is supposed to answer and deliver the message.

"Who is it?"

"Your wife."

I'm reading the chapter "There is a Solution" in the Big Book, a copy of which is given to everyone on arrival, and I set it down. I get up out of bed. I walk to the payphone. Being separated from my boys and Paula is lonely and painful, so I'm all the more happy to hear her voice. "I wanted to catch you before lights out." No calls are allowed after ten, and the rule is strictly enforced by the night staff. "I just checked your e-mail and Janet Fitch gave you a really nice blurb for The Los Angeles Diaries. I thought you'd like to hear it."

She reads it to me.

Like most artists, I'm starved for praise and confirmation, and since those moments are so far and few between I like to linger on them when they come. So Paula reads it again, and I let the words settle in. What I've always wanted most from my writing is critical acceptance and this quote means a lot to me. I am flattered. I am relieved.

"Can you thank her for me?"

"I already have."

But then another thought occurs to me.

"Does Janet know where I'm at?"

"I didn't mention it."

Paula has been answering my e-mails since I've been "on vacation," pretending she is me. It's a small lie compared to the irony and hypocrisy of having written a memoir where I intimate achieving sobriety when here I am hospitalized for alcoholism and other disorders of the mind. To call it bad timing is an understatement, and I feel like a fraud.

Paula lowers her voice.

"But I did have to tell your agent."

"What?"

"She called four times this week. What was I supposed to do?"

"I don't know but you didn't need to tell her I'm in a psycho rehab when I have this book coming out. I'm supposed to be clean and sober."

"Don't take it like that," Paula says. "She was very understanding and concerned. She was worried I might leave you."

"Well?"

"Quit acting stupid. I love you, you idiot. I just called to make you feel better."

A nurse is standing down the hall, staring at me, her arms crossed over her chest. "I better go," I say. "They give you little check-marks in this place for breaking the house rules, and if you get too many I don't know what happens. I think they waterboard you." I also feel the Seroquel kicking in, I'm getting drowsy, and soon my tongue will swell, making my words garbled and unintelligible. It's only a matter of minutes before I won't be able to talk, and navigating my way down the hall back to bed will present an almost hallucinogenic-like challenge.

Alone in my room again, I pick up where I left off in the Big Book, knowing that it won't be long before the sentences bleed together and I'm unable to read. The book quotes philosopher William James from *The Varieties of Religious Experience*, and Swiss psychiatrist Carl Jung, who suggests that for the recovery of a real alcoholic or addict a "huge emotional displacement must be made," and he predicates the success of this displacement for the seemingly doomed on a "vital spiritual experience." But how does that happen? How can you make it happen? What hope is there for the non-believer? The words on the page grow fuzzy, and with no answers to my questions, I turn off the bed lamp.

* * *

I'm five or six years old and I've just learned that my mother has been arrested and jailed. My brother and sister have locked themselves in their rooms, our father is drinking at the kitchen table straight from the bottle, and I wander outside and sit on the front lawn. I've been baptized Lutheran, our family attends the local Lutheran church, and I once believed in God. I once believed He could've saved my mother and did not. Looking up into the sky, I curse God.

From this night on, and for nearly the next forty years, I conclude that if there is a God, he's a cruel one and will never be of any use to me. That our mother deserves imprisonment doesn't cross the mind of this child, for he is only a child, incapable of understanding what is just and what is not and why.

In my heart, I carry hatred and anger deep into my adult years. On the streets, wasted on drugs and booze, I have no use for God.

My God is the bottle.

My God is in the sting of needle and the promise of escape as the plunger descends.

My God serves up a lifetime of guilt, alcohol, and dope. My God allows the good and innocent to die and the bad and evil to prosper. My God drags my boy through the ghettos of San Bernardino in a drunken, manic haze. My God is me and I do not forget. I do not forgive, and because I cannot forgive my brother or sister or anyone else who ever hurt me, I cannot forgive myself. For my cowardice. For my failure to act. For the cruel and hurtful things I've done to those I love.

I am afraid, when I leave the safe confines of this hospital, that I will return to my old ways, what alcoholics and addicts in A.A. and N.A. call going out, and that fear increases as the day of my release nears.

I arrived with a suitcase that was thoroughly checked for drugs and alcohol and potentially dangerous items, like razor blades or scissors, and I leave with that same suitcase, containing only what I originally brought: clothes and underwear, a toothbrush, some other toiletries. Paula is supposed to pick me up at two in the afternoon, but there is some kind of mix-up and the nurse comes for me at one. I don't mention the mistake.

She has a clipboard. Attached to it are several forms, one releasing the hospital of any liability once I leave the premises. It's signed by my psychiatrist, as are the others. I don't read them. I just scribble my signature in all the necessary places and pass the clipboard back to the nurse.

She smiles.

"You'll be okay," she says. "Just keep doing what you're doing and make sure you get to ninety meetings in ninety days.

Read your Big Book. Get a sponsor right away and work the Steps."

I don't know how many times I've been given that same advice, here, and before, in meetings I've attended on my own. She walks me to the end of the hall and then goes into an office.

"Good luck," she says. "I'll buzz you out."

The buzzer sounds. The steel doors through which I entered several weeks before swing open, and I step into the waiting room. The doors, heavy ones like those of a prison, shut behind me. I hear the lock slam into place.

A few days from now, Orlando will visit, and when we're alone, he'll tell me that I need to understand one thing—and understand it well.

"It's not your fault. None of it. Your brother, your sister, even Heidi. They're responsible for their own actions."

His mother dies while he's driving me and my boy home from the Hilton. He misses her last breath. He misses holding her hand and saying he loves her, and in that sacrifice he makes for me, as I accumulate more and more sober days, I will come to recognize it for what it is, the truest of gifts, an act of love and selflessness.

Outside the hospital, clouds move across the sky. For a short while it is sunny and warm. Then it turns gray and cool. I set my suitcase down and sit on the patch of lawn near the entrance to the parking lot. My wife will be here soon. I just have to be patient.

I watch the leaves of a tree move in a soft wind. I feel the dampness of the lawn through my jeans. The skin of my wrists itch from the blades of grass. She'll smile when she pulls into the lot and spots me. I'll return it. Then I'll get to my feet and walk straight and assuredly toward her. My eyes are clear. My hands are steady. I feel healthy and alert and fully intend to stay this way. I will attend meetings daily. I will get a sponsor. I will diligently work the Twelve Steps of Alcoholics Anonymous.

The man she will see is not the one who risked the life of his son leaping from a moving car. This man will kiss his wife when she arrives, and as they drive away from this hospital for the disturbed, he'll look out the window. In it, he will glimpse the reflection of a hopeful man firmly determined to stay sober. In it, he will also glimpse what is burrowed deep inside his other self, the alcoholic, the addict, always waiting to reemerge.

ACKNOWLEDGEMENTS

For this book I'm indebted to my terrific agent, Ryan Fischer-Harbage, and Dan Smetanka, the best book editor I've ever had. To my family, with all my love, I thank Paula, Andy, Logan and Nate. For their friendship, I thank Juan Delgado, Frank Ferro, Chet H., Art Monterastelli, Manuel Palacios, Gary S., and the fellowship of the Blue Jay Alano Club. Special appreciation goes to Orlando Ramirez who along with his help, loyalty and support, also lived a few of these stories.